Child Abuse and Neglect

Bassim Hamadeh, CEO and Publisher
John Remington, Senior Field Acquisitions Editor
Michelle Piehl, Senior Project Editor
Berenice Quirino, Associate Production Editor
Jess Estrella, Senior Graphic Designer
Stephanie Kohl, Licensing Associate
Natalie Piccotti, Director of Marketing
Kassie Graves, Vice President of Editorial
Jamie Giganti, Director of Academic Publishing

ISBN: 978-1-5165-2396-2 (pbk) / 978-1-5165-2397-9 (br)

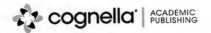

cognella® | ACADEMIC PUBLISHING

Child Abuse and Neglect

Mandated Reporting and Working with Child Survivors

First Edition

Julia A. Baxter

State University of New York at Oneonta

cognella® | ACADEMIC PUBLISHING

Table of Contents

Chapter 1

Child Abuse and Neglect

Julia A. Baxter

HISTORY OF CHILD PROTECTION IN AMERICA

People like to think of childhood as carefree days full of youthful fun and adventure. As adults, these days are often looked back on with nostalgia for the simplicity of youth. However, for many children both past and present, nothing could be further from the truth. In the past, being a child was fraught with peril on a daily basis. For some children today, it still is. According to Myers (2008), the history of child protection in America can be divided into three distinct time periods, the first of which would extend from colonial times to the beginning of formal (although nongovernmental) child protection organizations (then called societies) and practices.

Early in United States history there was an extensive time period during which children were seen as their family's property and fathers had the power to determine the manner in which his children were cared for; chillingly, he also had the right to determine if his child lived or died (Crosson-Tower, 2005). Eighteenth and nineteenth century America saw corporal punishment in both the home and classroom as the best way to raise children. Discipline was often severe, as children were meant to be obedient to God and parents. This was supported by theologian John Calvin's thought that a child's will must be broken in order for their sprit to be saved (Crosson-Tower, 2005). Beyond harsh discipline, the Industrial Revolution created a rise in child labor. Children worked long hours in harsh conditions. Many died as a result. However, since children were still seen as property and could be beaten, otherwise abused, or disregarded completely, being sent to work was often seen as a good lot in life.

History is full of incidents of sexual abuse and exploitation. As property of the father, girls, in early history, were frequently utilized by them as a means of currency. Daughters were employed by fathers to gain favor in business, and to increase land holdings or wealth. During the Victorian era, pornography and child prostitution were on the rise (Crosson-Tower, 2005). This is, sadly, a characteristic of this era as well. The contradictory nature of societal messages regarding children and sexuality were aptly noted by Crosson-Tower (2005),

> On one hand, we state that children should not be exploited sexually; on the other hand, child pornography thrives, both in print and on the Internet, and the courts are often more likely to believe molesting adults than molested children. Television commercials use nubile girls posed seductively. The Internet provides an excellent vehicle for perpetrators to contact children for sex. Such practices can only give molesters and children a mixed message about what society believes about sexual abuse and the sexual exploitation of children. (p. 8)

The first rape conviction in the history of California made it to the California Supreme Court in 1856. The case's victim was only thirteen years old; in fact, most rape appeals in California from 1856 to 1940 involved child victims (Myers, 2008).

The interventions to protect children from heinous abuse in these early days of American history were both intermittent and largely inadequate. However, there are documented cases of prosecution of offenders in the 1600s and 1700s. There was no organized child protection until the creation of the New York Society for the Prevention of Cruelty to Children, or SPCC in 1875 (Crosson-Tower, 2005, Myers, 2008). It must be noted, sadly, that the creation of the SPCC came after that of the Society for the Prevention of Cruelty to Animals (SPCA). The SPCA was established first in England in 1824 because activists wanted to protect carriage horses from abuse by their drivers and owners (spca.org, n.d.). The first American branch of the SPCA was established in New York in 1866. Many people with whom I have shared that fact are shocked that animal protection preceded child protection in America; however, many others are not at all surprised. There is an historical connection between the New York Branch of the SPCA and the creation of the SCCA in 1875 and a man named Henry Bergh.

The emergence of this first child protection society was a result of the abuse of Mary Ellen Wilson in 1874. Mary Ellen lived in a horrible tenement in New York City under the guardianship of Francis and Mary Connelly. She was the illegitimate daughter of the first husband of Mrs. Connelly. According to Crosson-Tower (2005) the poorly dressed eight-year-old girl was frequently observed by neighbors "shivering outside a locked door"; however, it was "Mary Ellen's screams as she was beaten with a leather strap" that prompted a neighbor to report the abuse and neglect to a Methodist mission worker named Etta who was resolute in her desire to save the young girl (p.11). This determination led her first to the police, who did not investigate the abuse, and then to charities whose charge was to help children, but who lacked any authority to intervene. According to Myers (2008), Wheeler eventually sought advice from Henry Bergh, who was the founder and president of the New York American Society of Cruelty to Animals. Bergh consulted his lawyer, Elbridge Gerry, who assisted him in finding a means by which Mary Ellen could be removed from her home. It was Bergh and Gerry who saw the glaring lack of any agency for child protection in America. As a result of Mary Ellen's abuse, they worked together to create the first charitable organization to focus on child protection and in 1875 The New York Society for the Prevention of Cruelty to Children (NYSPCC) came into being (Myers, 2008). Under the leadership of Attorney Gerry, The NYSPCC "began an impressive movement toward protecting children" (Crosson-Tower, 2005, p. 11). This dedicated organization is still vital today. A statement of their past and current missions can be found on their website.

> Founded in 1875, The New York Society for the Prevention of Cruelty to Children (NYSPCC) is the first child protective agency in the world. Throughout its 140-year history, The NYSPCC has sought, through the development of new and innovative programs, to meet the urgent needs of New York City's most vulnerable children. It is with this same spirit of innovation, concern and compassion that The NYSPCC responds to the complex needs of abused and neglected children, and those involved in their care, by providing best practice counseling, legal and educational services. (NYSPCC.org, n.d.)

This was the beginning of the child protection movement in America. Other branches of the SPCC were formed, and with them, greater protections for not only children who were abused, but also for those in severe poverty or who were victims of domestic violence. The move into the next era of child protection was in full swing.

From the creation of that first branch of the SPCC, much focus was given to not only child protection, but also to family assistance. In 1909, the White House held the Conference on Dependent Children, which in turn, lent support to the creation of a Federal Children's Bureau to oversee child welfare, which was created in 1912 (Crosson-Tower, 2005). By the 1920's, there were over 300 child protection societies in America (Myers, 2008). It must be noted, however, that these were nongovernmental agencies. As the twentieth century progressed, these private societies increasingly cried out for change in the form of increased governmental protection of children. Concurrently, the creation of state and federal agencies to provide social services was on the rise. With the advent of the Great Depression, a decline in privately funded agencies occurred as donations dried up due to a devastated economy. President Roosevelt's New Deal in 1935 included the Social Security Act, which created Aid to Dependent Children which provided financial assistance to children in low-income families. It also mandated the creation of child welfare services to provide for the protection of children who were dependent, homeless, neglected, or in danger of becoming delinquent (Crosson-Tower, 2005, Myers, 2008).

While federal and state governments were in the beginning stages of providing child protection services, nongovernmental child protection agencies were on a rapid decline. By 1967, there were only ten SPCC's in the country, down from the early 1900s high of 300. The resultant drop in child protection services was not matched by new creation of agencies to provide similar assistance on the state level. This resulted in a gap in the services needed to ensure the protection of children's welfare. Many communities lacked the means to provide services for abused and neglected children. According to Myers

(2008) "for the first six decades of the twentieth century, protective services in most communities were inadequate, and in some places, nonexistent" (p. 454).

However, in the 1960s interest vastly increased in child abuse, sparked by an article published in 1946 by John Caffey, a radiology professor from Columbia University. Caffey's paper reviewed cases of young children with limb fractures and subdural hematomas that were not adequately explained by caregivers. While his paper insinuated the possibility that these children were abused, it did not state it blatantly (Myers, 2008). What followed was a steady parade of physicians who also studied such cases. In 1962, Dr. Henry Kemp and his colleagues published the article, "The Battered-Child Syndrome" in the *Journal of the American Medical Association*, giving the condition a name. According to Crosson-Tower (2005), this label referred to a "condition in young children who had apparently been victims of severe physical abuse, generally at the hands of a parent or foster parent" (p. 12). This now famous publication brought child abuse to the forefront of national attention, ushering in the modern era of child protection (Myers, 2008).

Dr. Kemp became a leader in the fight to have a formal system for the reporting of child abuse. Articles were published in widely read national magazines that supported Dr. Kemp's sentiment that "The battered child syndrome isn't a reportable disease, but it damn well ought to be" (Myers, 2008, p. 454). Congress created amendments to the Social Security Act in 1962 which focused on child protection. From 1963 to 1967, all U. S. states and the District of Columbia passed laws requiring the reporting of child abuse. These statutes were known as *mandatory reporting* laws, and required specific professionals, such as doctors and teachers, to report suspected cases of child abuse and neglect to the appropriate authorities (findlaw.com, n.d.). In 1972, The National Center for the Prevention of Child Abuse and Neglect was instituted to provide information on these topics to professionals. In 1973, The Child Abuse Prevention Bill was put forth under the sponsorship of then Senator Walter Mondale (Crosson-Tower, 2005). This movement culminated in the creation of the first federal law to establish child abuse reporting guidelines: The Child Abuse Prevention and Treatment Act of 1974, or CAPTA (Child Welfare Information Gateway, 2011). CAPTA authorized the use of federal funding to strengthen the state agencies whose charge it was to respond to child abuse, neglect, and sexual abuse; it also provided funds for training and was tasked with the improvement of both the investigation and reporting processes. CAPTA has been renewed by Congress periodically, and is still in force today. By the end of the 1970s America finally had a nationwide system of government supported child protection in place, which encompassed abuse, neglect, and child sexual abuse (Myers, 2008).

The 1980s was a decade of increased interest in child abuse prevention and intervention in addition to trying to understand its root causes and subsequent consequences. To address this, as well as to focus on the plight of children in the foster care system, congress passed the Adoption Assistance and Child Welfare Act of 1980. The purpose of this legislation was to require states to make "reasonable efforts to avoid removing children from maltreating parents" and if removal proved necessary to make "reasonable efforts to return the child home or move toward termination of parental rights" (Myers,

2008, p. 459). This concept of family preservation, still the foundation of many state child protection and foster care agencies today, is hotly debated with regard to ifs efficacy in protecting children. In addition to family preservation, targeted interventions became part of many programs in the 1980s. These included endeavors such as services to new parents, parenting education classes and support groups, crisis intervention services, hotlines to assist in reducing physical abuse and neglect, and education of children on ownership of their bodies and good touch versus bad or questionable touch (Child Welfare Information Gateway, 2011). While the intentions of parent education programs were noble, effectiveness was limited due to insufficient access and a lack of recognition of the need for assistance. Still, such programs were amazingly strong in comparison to what was available in the 1960s.

In the following decade, the establishment programs based on supporting every parent and child became the focus. Home-based interventions for pregnant women and newborn children became more popular, and this model demonstrated gains in parent-child attachment and positive child development. The Affordable Care Act of 2009 included a provision to provide states with $1.5 billion over five years to "expand the provision of evidence-based home visitation programs to at risk pregnant women and newborns" (Child Welfare Information Gateway, 2011, p.4). One continuing focus remains prevention strategies, especially those that are more broadly targeted. According to The Child Welfare Information Gateway (2011), some research suggests that these programs "have greater success in strengthening a parent's or a child's protective factors than in eliminating risk factors" (p. 5). Further, "a wide range of prevention strategies has demonstrated an ability to reduce child abuse and neglect reports as well as other child safety outcomes such as reported injuries and accidents" (Brief/prevention, p.5). Some of these strategies include greater public awareness efforts, child sexual assault prevention classes, parent education and support groups, home visitation programs, and community prevention efforts.

It is clear by review of this brief history of child maltreatment prevention that there have been enormous strides made since the 1960s. The creation of child protective services and their availability nationwide in the 1970s was a savior for hundreds of children who were being victimized or neglected by their parents and caregivers. On a personal note, as a child victim of an abusive parent in the 50s and early 60s, I found it shocking to learn that there was no protection available for me during that time period. Like so many in my generation, excessive physical and emotional abuse in the name of discipline was something I endured. One of my earliest memories entails my mother being held at gunpoint by my father and my sister and I running to the neighbors for help. That help came in the form of the police, who took the gun from my father and told him to "go sleep it off". Even at the age of four I knew that something wasn't right about that scenario. The truth is that scenes such as this were occurring all over America. Abused women and children had no recourse other than to stay in these difficult situations and try to survive. Ironically, as child protection services continued to increase and serve children all over the country, those working in the field were inundated with reports of suspected abuse and neglect. The sheer number of reports began to overwhelm the agencies which were responsible for dealing with them and by the 1980s, the system was struggling to keep up (Myers, 2008). This continues today, unfortunately. There never seems to be enough resources available to meet the overwhelming needs of these children. While today's system of child protection is certainly less than perfect, it is a far cry from being left alone to endure mental, emotional, and physical pain on a daily basis with no hope for intervention. When I hear education and counseling professionals bemoan the failings of the current system and use them as an excuse to do nothing to intervene, it is that four -year-old girl in me that speaks back to them. You must. We all must. You have no idea the difference this could make in a child's life.

SCOPE OF THE PROBLEM

Have you ever been to a football game in a professional stadium or seen one on television? Close your eyes and picture the size of the stadium empty. See all of the empty seats; there are thousands of them. Now imagine them filled with children who have been abused and neglected. That is a tough picture to imagine. If you put ten football stadiums side by side and filled them with these children, you would have an accurate picture of the approximate number of children who are abused and neglected in the United States in one year. In 2014, state agencies reported about 702,000 victims of child maltreatment (nationalchildrensalliance.org, 2016). That would easily fill these football stadiums. Unfortunately, that would not tell the entire story of the extent of this problem in America. The truth is that the majority of children who are abused, neglected or otherwise maltreated never come to the attention of those government agencies charged with protecting them.

Children may show no outward signs of abuse or neglect, making it hard to detect. Particularly underreported are cases of sexual abuse. The reasons for this are numerous, and include feelings of shame, secrecy, and fear; all of these may prevent a child from looking for help. So, when we see child abuse numbers, such as the ones above, what can be said of such statistics? Clinical psychologist Dr. Hopper suggested that "official government statistics do not indicate actual rates of child abuse" (Hopper, J., 2018, Sources of Statistics, Para. 3). Hopper also noted that "government statistics are based on cases that were (a) reported to social service agencies, (b) investigated by child protection workers, and (c) had sufficient evidence to determine that a legal definition of 'abuse' or 'neglect' was met" (Sources of Statistics, Para. 4). The ten football stadiums we previously pictured filled with children, then, do not offer us a complete picture at all.

About three million reports of child abuse are made in the United States each year and may involve as many as six million children (childhelp.org, n.d.). According to the National Children's Alliance (2013/2014), in 2013, forty-seven states reported that approximately 3.1 million children had received intervention from Child Protective Services (CPS) agencies in the U.S; children under one year of age had the highest rate of victimization. Of those receiving services, approximately 80% suffered neglect, 18% were victims of physical abuse, 9% were sexual abuse victims, and 8.7% were psychologically maltreated (nationalchildrensalliance.org, n.d.). The reality is that a report of child abuse or neglect is made about every ten seconds in America. While you were reading this, several more reports have been made.

An excellent source of information regarding the statistics of child abuse and neglect in America is the Child Maltreatment Report generated by the Department of Health and Human Services every year. The most recent report contains statistics from 2014 nationally and by state. While exact statistics are not the issue here, they give a startling picture of the scope of this problem. The key findings of this report can be summarized as follows (acf.gov, 2016).

In 2010 the national estimates of children receiving some response from CPS was 3,023,000. This figure rose to 3,248,000 in 2014, representing a 7.4% increase. The number of child victims increased from 698,000 in 2010 to 702,000 in 2014. Figure 1.1 demonstrates the large variation between reported cases and actual child victims. The largest two columns indicate the number of total referrals made in 2014, and the total number of children referred during that year. This is a good visualization of the actual number of children found to be victims of child abuse and neglect versus the total number of children referred during the same period. The graph indicates the enormous amount of work state and local agencies do to screen, refer, investigate, and act on cases of child abuse and neglect every year. It bears keeping in mind when the lack of perceived action by these agencies becomes frustrating. They are often overwhelmed and frequently work at or above full capacity.

Another key finding of the 2014 Child Maltreatment Report is that nationally, an estimated 1,580 children died as a result of abuse or neglect. That rate represents 2.13 children per 100,000 children in our country. This means that more than 4 (4.3) children

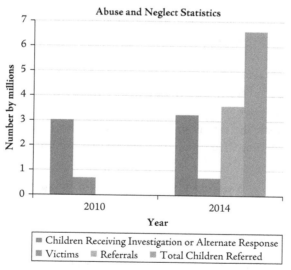

FIGURE 1.1   Abuse and Neglect Statistics

Figure 1.1 compares the number of children receiving investigation or response from CPS and actual victims in 2010 and 2014. Referrals and total children referred to CPS are represented for 2014. Source: Administration for Children & Families, 2014. Published January 25, 2016.

per day die in America from abuse and neglect. This number has ranged from a low of 3.6 in 2000 to a high of 4.8 in 2009. The president of the Every Child Matters Education Fund (ECM), Michael Petit, made this statement about the numbers:

> Over the past 10 years more than 20,000 American children are believed to have been killed in their own homes by family members. That is nearly four times the number of U.S. soldiers killed in Iraq and Afghanistan. The child maltreatment death rate in the US is triple Canada's and 11 times that of Italy. (Petit, 2011, Para. 1)

It is sad to note that studies have shown the United States to have the worst record of child maltreatment deaths among other western industrialized countries. Additionally, as is true with all numbers connected with abuse and neglect, it is widely believed that these numbers are also undercounted. The true number of deaths may in fact be much greater. The ECM Fund (2012) paid tribute to some of these children. Known cases of child death due to abuse and neglect were indicated by state and included the names and causes of death for many children. The children ranged from one month to 13 years of age. Causes of death were chilling, and included beating, shaking, skull fracture, strangulation, starvation, dehydration, drowning, head trauma, asphyxiation from being bound with tape, overdose of medication, blunt force trauma, and torture (p. 216). The majority of child deaths occur in children under the age of 3 and more than 80% were not yet old enough for kindergarten (childhelp.org, n.d.). Boys had a higher child fatality rate than girls. Interestingly, almost 90% of fatalities were comprised of three ethnicities: White (43%), African-American (43%) and Hispanic (15.1%) (nationalchildrensalliance.org, n.d.).

Children in their first year of life account for the highest rate of victimization overall (nationalchildrensalliance.org, n.d.), but age is only one risk factor. Below are some noted risk factors for child abuse and neglect (childwelfare.gov., 2004). It is important, though, to remember that this list is not all-inclusive, nor do the risk factors imply causality. Each case of child maltreatment is unique, and incidents of child abuse and neglect can be found in a myriad of situations defying all statistical tendencies. Please remember in your work with children that child victims of abuse can be any gender, age, race, ethnicity, socioeconomic status, and family structure. No child can be seen as immune from this risk. While viewing these lists of risk factors, please keep this in mind.

COMMON CHILD ABUSE AND NEGLECT RISK FACTORS

Common Child Risk Factors

- Premature birth, birth anomalies, low birth weight, exposure to toxins in utero
- Temperament: difficult or slow to warm up
- Physical, cognitive, or emotional disability, or chronic or serious illness
- Antisocial peer group
- Age (statistically, the younger the child, the greater the risk)
- Child aggression, behavior problems, attention deficits

Common Parental or Family Risk Factors

- Personality Factors
  - External locus of control
  - Poor impulse control
  - Depression or anxiety
  - Low tolerance for frustration
  - Feelings of insecurity
  - Lack of trust
- Insecure attachment with own parents
- Childhood history of abuse
- High parental conflict, domestic violence
- Family structure—single parent with lack of support, high number of children in household
- Social isolation, lack of support
- Parental psychopathology
- Substance abuse
- Separation or divorce, especially high conflict divorce
- Age (statistically, the younger the parent(s), the greater the risk)
- High general stress level
- Poor parent-child interaction, negative attitudes, and attributions about child's behavior
- Inaccurate knowledge and expectations about child development

Social and Environmental Risk Factors

- Low socioeconomic status
- Stressful life events
- Lack of access to medical care, health insurance, adequate child care, and social services
- Parental unemployment; homelessness
- Social isolation or lack of social support
- Exposure to racism or discrimination
- Poor schools
- Exposure to environmental toxins
- Dangerous or violent neighborhood
- Community violence

When I entered teaching and then counseling, I felt that it was my duty to keep an eye on the poor rural children who lived on isolated farms or in crowded and dirty trailer parks. Colleagues of mine in big cities were mindful of children from certain neighborhoods. While poverty, single parent households, unemployment, and neighborhood are some statistical risk factors for abuse and neglect, they are by no means predictive. I have worked with many children from families demonstrating all of those factors who were loved and well cared for. Conversely, I have seen or heard of incidents of serious child maltreatment in families that one might overlook due to a variety of reasons. Some were the children of doctors, lawyers, and area business owners, some were being raised in beautiful homes in high income areas, and some were children of local teachers. The point to remember here is that you cannot presume that children are at higher risk just because they live in a common at-risk situation or that they are lower risk because they don't. Each possible incident of child abuse and neglect must be considered individually. I always tell my students to go with their gut feelings. This is truly not a one size fits all situation.

On a more positive note, there are protective factors for children as well, and many of them are important to remember as professionals who work with children. Some things that you may want to work on with your students and young clients are developing hobbies and interests, developing good peer relationships, and increasing self-esteem, coping skills, and social skills (childwelfare.gov 2004). As individuals who work on the front lines with children, it is easy to become discouraged. Always remember that there are many things you can do to help. Being a supportive adult or mentor to a child is viewed as a protective factor in its own right.

DEFINITIONS AND CATEGORIES

> There are several types of child abuse, but the core element that ties them together is the emotional effect on the child. Children need predictability, structure, clear boundaries, and the knowledge that their parents are looking out for their safety. Abused children cannot predict how their parents will act. Their world is an unpredictable, frightening place with no rules. Whether the abuse is a slap, a harsh comment, stony silence, or not knowing if there will be dinner on the table tonight, the end result is a child that feels unsafe, uncared for, and alone. (HelpGuide.org, 2016)

Raising children is a difficult endeavor for most people. A child's needs are many: food, shelter, love, play, clothing, and medical care, just to name a few. Although caregivers might want to provide a child all of the above things, not all parents and caregivers are equally well equipped emotionally, physically, mentally, or financially to care for a child. Personal, psychological, and social stressors and pressures can prevent caregivers from being able to provide a child with what they need. While the adult may not intend to cause harm to the child for whom they are caring, they can become overwhelmed and angry. This high state of emotion may bring about a loss of control which could result in harm to the child. According to the American Psychological Association (2016), adults might harm children because they:

- lose their tempers when they think about their own problems,
- don't know how to discipline a child,

- expect behavior that is unrealistic for a child's age or ability,
- have been abused by a parent or a partner,
- have financial problems, or
- lose control when they use alcohol or other drugs. (Protecting our children from abuse—why do adults hurt children? APA.org).

Child maltreatment comes in many forms and has been labeled differently by various agencies and authors. In some reports, maltreatment is divided into three categories: neglect, physical abuse, and sexual abuse. In many cases, emotional maltreatment (also called psychological abuse or emotional neglect) is grouped with neglect, but sometimes it is considered separately.

As shown in Figure 1.2, neglect represents the largest percentage of cases, followed by physical abuse, and then sexual abuse. When you look at this, though, always keep in mind that sexual and emotional abuse very often go under reported. Other sources divide the categories further. A significant study undertaken by the Center for Disease Control and Prevention (CDC) and Kaiser Permanente (ACE Study, 1998) looked at the link between adverse child experiences and health and well-being later in life. Figure 1.3 shows their findings for the prevalence of reported abuse by category.

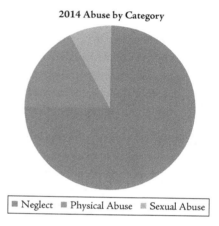

2014 Abuse by Category

■ Neglect ■ Physical Abuse ■ Sexual Abuse

FIGURE 1.2   2014 Abuse by Category

Source: Administration for Children & Families, 2014.

Prevalence of Reports by Category

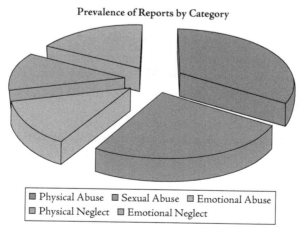

■ Physical Abuse ■ Sexual Abuse ■ Emotional Abuse
■ Physical Neglect ■ Emotional Neglect

FIGURE 1.3   Prevalence of Reports by Category

Source: ACE Study, 1998 (as cited in CDC.gov, 2016)

Regardless of wording or exact numbers, for the purpose of this text, we will divide type of abuse into four categories:

1. Physical Abuse
2. Neglect
3. Sexual Abuse
4. Emotional Maltreatment

Each section contains definitions and information regarding one of these categories of maltreatment, as well as what to look for to assist in recognition. Note that there is often more than one type of abuse happening in a child's life. As stated by Prevent Child Abuse America.org (n.d.),

> The first step in helping abused children is learning to recognize the symptoms of child abuse. Although child abuse is divided into four types … the types are more typically found in combination than alone. A physically abused child, for example, is often emotionally maltreated as well, and a sexually abused child may also be neglected. (Recognizing Child Abuse: What Parents Should Know, 2016, para. 1)

While the following information can be used by education, counseling, or other professionals as a resource to assist in identification of child abuse and neglect, it is by no means a checklist leading to the certainty of abuse. Every case is different, as every child and circumstance are different. Therefore, nothing can replace the professional's relationship with the child in question. Your instinct based on your knowledge and training is invaluable when facing a strong suspicion that abuse, neglect, or both have taken place. Bearing all of this in mind, the more one knows about the categories of child abuse and neglect, the greater the foundation from which to draw when trying to make a determination.

PHYSICAL ABUSE

> Carlos came home from work in a foul mood. Seven-year-old Miguel ran out of the kitchen just as his father walked in, and they ran into each other. Carlos cursed and grabbed his son. He shook Miguel hard while yelling at him and then shoved him out of the way. The next day, Miguel's arms and back had bruises. (APA.org, 2016, section 2, para. 1)

The above example is one of many possible scenarios in which a child could be physically abused. Abuse encompasses the most serious harms against children but is statistically far less prevalent than neglect. Some abuse is accidental due to anger and frustration, like the above example might be. Some abuse is more purposeful and can be seen as discipline in the eyes of the caregiver.

Federal legislation is the foundation of state law on child abuse and neglect and offers a definition that includes a minimum set of acts or behaviors to qualify as neglect or abuse. CAPTA, as amended and reauthorized by the CAPTA Reauthorization Act of 2010, defines child abuse and neglect as, at a minimum,

Any recent act or failure to act on the part of a parent or caretaker which results in death, serious physical or emotional harm, sexual abuse or exploitation; or an act or failure to act which presents an imminent risk of serious harm. (childwelfare.gov, n.d.)

It should be mentioned that most federal and state laws pertaining to child protection refer to the harm of a child being caused by a parent or other caregiver, and not that caused by strangers or acquaintances. These cases are seen as criminal acts, and are referred to law enforcement officials, and not to child protection service professionals.

The definition of physical abuse, according to The Child Welfare Information Gateway (childwelfare.gov) is:

Nonaccidental physical injury (ranging from minor bruises to severe fractures or death) as a result of punching, beating, kicking, biting, shaking, throwing, stabbing, choking, hitting (with a hand, stick, strap, or other object), burning, or otherwise harming a child, that is inflicted by a parent, caregiver, or other person who has responsibility for the child. Such injury is considered abuse regardless of whether the caregiver intended to hurt the child. (2016, p. 2)

The exact definition of physical abuse varies by state legislation, but to some degree, contains much of the above regardless of jurisdiction. Some states, such as New York, include actions that create a substantial risk of physical injury to the child as part of the definition. It is important to consult the exact laws in the state in which you work to know the exact definition and parameters that apply.

There are many sound resources available for gathering information on how to recognize child abuse and we list some in the references section of this book. The list below describes a large variety of warning signs in an inclusive and easy to read format. However, this list is by no means exhaustive. Experienced counselors, educators, and other professional child practitioners no doubt see signs like these, and many others that are not listed. It is, though, a good place to start learning how to identify child abuse (NOTE: All of the indicators in the next sections came from the following resources: U.S. Department of Health and Human Services [USDHHS]; Crosson-Tower, 2003; childwelfare.gov, July 2013; Prevent Child Abuse America, 2003; National Child Traumatic Stress Network [NCTSN], Oct. 2009; nj.gov/dcf, n.d.; ocfs.ny.gov, n.d.; americanspcc.org, n.d.; and helpguide.org, n.d. Please see the references and resources sections for more information).

Physical Indicators and Warning Signs of Abuse You Might Observe in the Child

Please note that one should pay particular attention to any injuries that are not explained, not in keeping with the explanation given by the parent or caretaker, or inconsistent with the child's developmental level.

Figure 1.4 depicts the major groups of physical indications of child abuse broken down into categories. Figures 1.5–1.8 provide a more detailed look at possible warning signs found in each category.

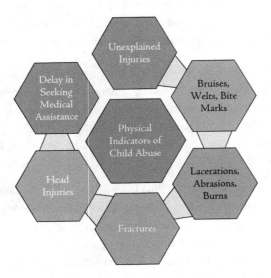

FIGURE 1.4   Physical Indicators and Warning Signs of Abuse You Might Observe in the Child

Source: Adapted from: USDHHS, Crosson-Tower, 2003; Children's Bureau, 2013; Prevent Child Abuse America, 2003; National Center for Child Traumatic Stress, 2009; New Jersey Department of Children and Families; Office of Children and Family Services, New York State; American Society for the Positive Care of Children; Helpguide.org

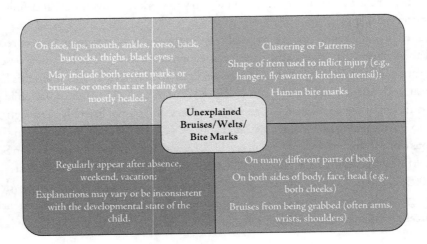

FIGURE 1.5   Detailed Warning Signs: Unexplained Welts, Bruises, Bite Marks

Source: Adapted from: USDHHS, Crosson-Tower, 2003; Children's Bureau, 2013; Prevent Child Abuse America, 2003; National Center for Child Traumatic Stress, 2009; New Jersey Department of Children and Families; Office of Children and Family Services, New York State; American Society for the Positive Care of Children; Helpguide.org.

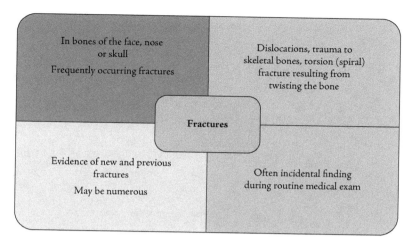

FIGURE 1.6   Detailed Warning Signs: Fractures

Source: Adapted from: USDHHS, Crosson-Tower, 2003; Children's Bureau, 2013; Prevent Child Abuse America, 2003; National Center for Child Traumatic Stress, 2009; New Jersey Department of Children and Families; Office of Children and Family Services, New York State; American Society for the Positive Care of Children; Helpguide.org.

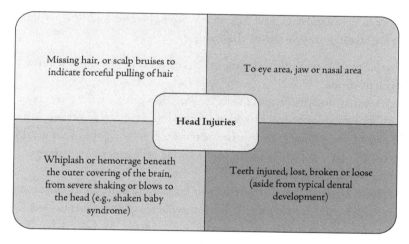

FIGURE 1.7   Detailed Warning Signs: Head Injuries

Source: Adapted from: USDHHS, Crosson-Tower, 2003; Children's Bureau, 2013; Prevent Child Abuse America, 2003; National Center for Child Traumatic Stress, 2009; New Jersey Department of Children and Families; Office of Children and Family Services, New York State; American Society for the Positive Care of Children; Helpguide.org.

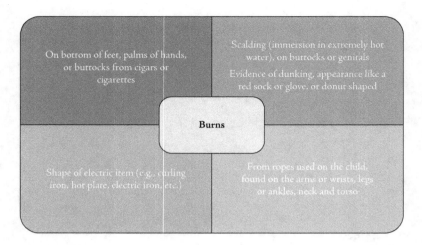

FIGURE 1.8   Detailed Warning Signs: Burns

Source: Adapted from: USDHHS, Crosson-Tower, 2003; Children's Bureau, 2013; Prevent Child Abuse America, 2003; National Center for Child Traumatic Stress, 2009; New Jersey Department of Children and Families; Office of Children and Family Services, New York State; American Society for the Positive Care of Children; Helpguide.org.

According to the National Child Traumatic Stress Network (2009) several additional indicators are strongly suggestive of child abuse.

- "Frequent physical injuries that are attributed to the child's being clumsy or accident-prone
- Injuries that do not seem to fit the explanation given by the parents or child
- Conflicting explanations provided by child and/or caregivers, explanations that do not fit the injuries, or injuries attributed to accidents that could not have occurred given the child's age (for example an immersion burn on a child too young to walk or crawl)
- Habitual absence from or lateness to school without credible reason. Parents may keep a child at home until physical evidence of abuse has healed. One should also be suspicious if a child comes to school wearing long-sleeved or high-collared clothing on hot days, since this may be an attempt to hide injuries
- Awkward movements or difficulty walking; this may suggest that the child is in pain or suffers from the aftereffects of repeated injuries" (Child Physical Abuse Fact Sheet, p. 2).

While the above list is startling, you may not see any physical signs of abuse in the children with whom you work. Remember, most parents and caregivers are aware that educators and mental health professionals are mandated to report child abuse and neglect by the states that license or certify them. Because of this, the adults can be very careful about sending children to school or other situations where trained reporters will have contact with their children. If you do not see any physical sign of abuse (which is often the case), there are many behavioral indicators that child abuse is present.

Behavioral Indicators or Warning Signs of Abuse You Might Observe in the Child

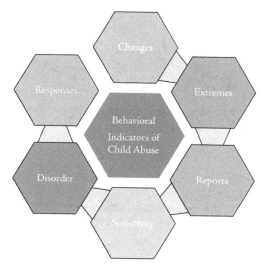

FIGURE 1.9   Behavioral Indicators or Warning Signs of Abuse You Might Observe in the Child

Source: Adapted from: USDHHS, Crosson-Tower, 2003; Children's Bureau, 2013; Prevent Child Abuse America, 2003; National Center for Child Traumatic Stress, 2009; New Jersey Department of Children and Families; Office of Children and Family Services, New York State; American Society for the Positive Care of Children; Helpguide.org.

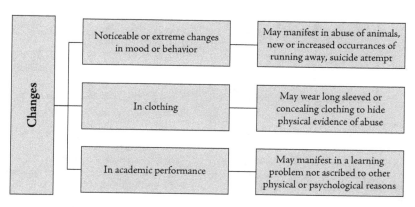

FIGURE 1.10   Changes

Source: Adapted from: USDHHS, Crosson-Tower, 2003; Children's Bureau, 2013; Prevent Child Abuse America, 2003; National Center for Child Traumatic Stress, 2009; New Jersey Department of Children and Families; Office of Children and Family Services, New York State; American Society for the Positive Care of Children; Helpguide.org.

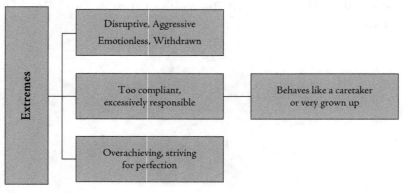

FIGURE 1.11   Extremes

Source: Adapted from: USDHHS, Crosson-Tower, 2003; Children's Bureau, 2013; Prevent Child Abuse America, 2003; National Center for Child Traumatic Stress, 2009; New Jersey Department of Children and Families; Office of Children and Family Services, New York State; American Society for the Positive Care of Children; Helpguide.org.

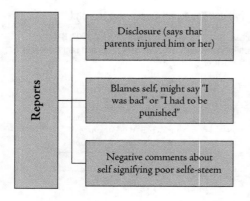

FIGURE 1.12   Reports

Source: Adapted from: USDHHS, Crosson-Tower, 2003; Children's Bureau, 2013; Prevent Child Abuse America, 2003; National Center for Child Traumatic Stress, 2009; New Jersey Department of Children and Families; Office of Children and Family Services, New York State; American Society for the Positive Care of Children; Helpguide.org.

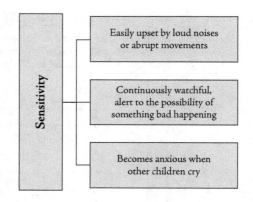

FIGURE 1.13   Sensitivity

Source: Adapted from: USDHHS, Crosson-Tower, 2003; Children's Bureau, 2013; Prevent Child Abuse America, 2003; National Center for Child Traumatic Stress, 2009; New Jersey Department of Children and Families; Office of Children and Family Services, New York State; American Society for the Positive Care of Children; Helpguide.org.

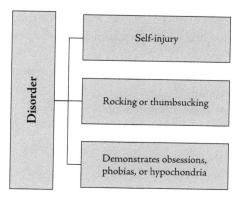

FIGURE 1.14 Disorder

Source: Adapted from: USDHHS, Crosson-Tower, 2003; Children's Bureau, 2013; Prevent Child Abuse America, 2003; National Center for Child Traumatic Stress, 2009; New Jersey Department of Children and Families; Office of Children and Family Services, New York State; American Society for the Positive Care of Children; Helpguide.org.

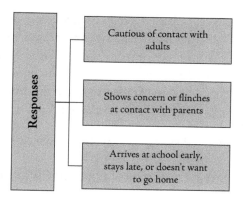

FIGURE 1.15 Responses

Source: Adapted from: USDHHS, Crosson-Tower, 2003; Children's Bureau, 2013; Prevent Child Abuse America, 2003; National Center for Child Traumatic Stress, 2009; New Jersey Department of Children and Families; Office of Children and Family Services, New York State; American Society for the Positive Care of Children; Helpguide.org.

Indicators or Warning Signs You Might Observe in the Parent or Caregiver:

While it is good to know the warning signs in children, parents or caregivers often demonstrate telltale indicators that there might be abuse (or the potential thereof) at home. The Mayo Clinic's Child and Family Advocacy Center offered some suggestions of what to look for (mayoclinic.org, n.d.).

+ Adult may have experienced abuse as a child
+ Evidence of abuse of pets or other animals (e.g., hits the dog, kicks the cat)
+ May portray the child in a very negative light (such as "what did the little idiot do now?"); may refer to the child as bad, evil, useless, or a burden
+ Demonstrates a lack of concern for the child
+ Inability to see and acknowledge the child's distress (emotional or physical)
+ Denies difficulties at home or attributes them to child
+ Uses severe physical discipline at home or suggests that teachers or other caregivers do the same in the event of bad behavior
+ Expects level of performance academically or physically that is developmentally inappropriate or impossible to attain (*I once had a student whose mother wanted her to be thinner so that she would look just like and just as beautiful as the mother. However, even at nine years of age, this child was already taller and had a bigger frame than her mother. The child was being asked to do something that would never have been physically possible.*)

- Isolates the child from others or sets strong limits on who they can interact with and for how long; may give reasons for keeping the child from others such as punishment, or focus on the child needing to study more, etc.
- Expects the child to give attention to the adult or take care of the adult; may appear jealous of others to whom the child gives attention
- Explanations for the child's injuries are absent, don't make sense, or are conflicting

(mayoclinic.org, n.d.; childwelfare.gov, 2007; Child Abuse America, 2003)

Some Examples of Physical Child Abuse

1. Shaking or shoving
2. Biting, kicking, or punching
3. Cutting with a sharp object
4. Slapping or hitting
5. Beating with a belt, shoe, or other object
6. Burning with matches or cigarettes
7. Scalding with extremely hot water
8. Pulling hair out
9. Breaking an arm, leg, or other bone
10. Withholding food, drink, or bathroom use

NEGLECT

> John worked nights at the grocery store, but the family needed more money. Ellen looked for work, but the only job she could find required her to leave home at 3 a.m. The children, ages two and six, were alone for a few hours until John got home. (APA.org, section 5, para. 1)

Neglect is by far the most prevalent form of child maltreatment, accounting for over three-quarters of confirmed cases of child maltreatment in the United States. Neglect includes acts of omission; in other words, the failure of the caregivers to provide for the child's basic needs, such as food, clothing, shelter, schooling, affection, hygiene, or supervision (helpguide.org, 2016; kidsmatterinc.org, n.d.). The Child Welfare Information Gateway (2011a) offers this definition:

> The failure of a parent or other person with responsibility for the child to provide needed food, clothing, shelter, medical care, or supervision to the degree that the child's health, safety, and well-being are threatened with harm. (p. 2)

Some state statutes are quite specific about classifications of neglect, which can include medical neglect, educational neglect, abandonment, and others. Additionally, some states explicitly exempt certain circumstances for the determination of neglect such as religious exemptions for medical neglect and financial considerations for physical neglect (Child Welfare Information Gateway, 2011b). Definitions of neglect are inconsistent though, due to what can be seen as ambiguous situations and the various ways in which a child can be neglected.

Despite the inconsistencies among state laws, the most commonly recognized types of neglect can be summarized as follows (Child Welfare Information Gateway, 2012, p. 3).

+ Physical neglect: Abandoning the child or refusing to accept custody; not providing for basic needs like nutrition, hygiene, appropriate clothing, or housing
+ Medical neglect: Delaying or denying recommended health care for the child
+ Inadequate supervision: Leaving the child unsupervised (depending on length of time and child's age and maturity); not protecting the child from safety hazards, providing inadequate caregivers, or engaging in harmful behavior
+ Emotional neglect: Isolating the child; not providing affection or emotional support; exposing the child to domestic violence or substance abuse
+ Educational neglect: Failing to enroll the child in school or homeschool; ignoring special education needs; permitting chronic absenteeism from school

Neglect can be the result of a temporary inattention to a need or situation, to deprivation that is chronic, or and worse yet, willful. Parents or caregivers may be incapable of caring for a child's needs due to extreme poverty, physical or mental illness, substance abuse, parenting and family stress, or domestic violence. Those are only a few possible risk factors, and neglect can take place in the absence of such risk factors as well. Instances of parents who work many hours and have been neglectful of their children are not found only in low socioeconomic situations. The risk in higher income brackets is there as well. Parents or caregivers driven to succeed who focus on work all the time may also be neglectful. As noted earlier, it is always important to remember that instances of abuse and neglect have been recorded across all socioeconomic, ethnic, religious, cultural, and educational backgrounds.

Outward signs of neglect may be difficult to see, even for trained professional. Older children, particularly, may be adept at presenting a positive image on the outside. While the neglected child may be more difficult to spot than the abused child, child neglect can be exemplified by physical, behavioral, and emotional characteristics.

Physical Indicators or Warning Signs of Neglect You Might Observe in the Child

FIGURE 1.16   Physical Indicators of Neglect

Source: Adapted from: USDHHS, Crosson-Tower, 2003; Children's Bureau, 2013; Prevent Child Abuse America, 2003; National Center for Child Traumatic Stress, 2009; New Jersey Department of Children and Families; Office of Children and Family Services, New York State; American Society for the Positive Care of Children; Helpguide.org.

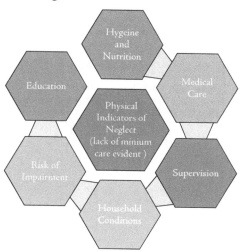

| Personal Hygeine Nutrition | Indications that the child's physical needs are being left unattended |

+ Poor care of teeth, skin, hair, body; consistent odor, insect bites, consistently dirty and unbathed, matted hair, etc.
+ Persistent hunger; inadequate quality or availability of nutritious food at home, lack of prepared meals, usafe food present in home (spoilage)

| Supervison | Indications that the child is not well supervised or left alone for long periods of time regularly |

+ Unsupervised engagement in dangerous activities
+ States no one is at home (abandonment)
+ Evidence of poor supervision might include numerous falls, ingestion of household toxins, left in a car unattended, alone outside/on street, child reports being caretaker of others (performs as parent)

| Risk of Impairment | Indications that the child's environment may provide risks to the child's appropriate growth and wellbeing |

+ Evident speech disorder
+ Physical development delay
+ Clothing is not appropriate for the weather, is filthy or ill-fitting

| Medical Care | Indications that the child's medical care needs are not being met |

+ Physical, dental, emotional problems in need of medical attention are being ignored
+ Failure to thrive is evident medically or emotionally
+ Evidence of toxicology in a newborn or child

| Household Conditions | Indications that the child is living in an unsafe environement |

+ Unsanitary environment (insect infestations, animal or human excrement, garbage)
+ Lack of heat, clean water, or hot water
+ Condemned housing, unsafe and/or dirty sleeping conditions, fire hazards, hoarding

| Education | Indications that the child's need for education is being ignored or unmet |

+ Often misses school
+ Often arrives late to school ·

FIGURE 1.17   Detailed Warning Signs of Neglect

Source: Adapted from: USDHHS, Crosson-Tower, 2003; Children's Bureau, 2013; Prevent Child Abuse America, 2003; National Center for Child Traumatic Stress, 2009; New Jersey Department of Children and Families; Office of Children and Family Services, New York State; American Society for the Positive Care of Children; Helpguide.org.

Behavioral Indicators or Warning Signs of Neglect You Might Observe in the Child

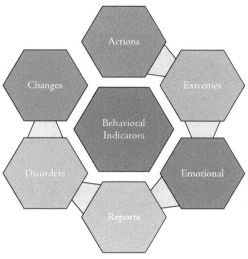

FIGURE 1.18   Behavioral Indicators or Warning Signs of Neglect

Source: Adapted from: USDHHS, Crosson-Tower, 2003; Children's Bureau, 2013; Prevent Child Abuse America, 2003; National Center for Child Traumatic Stress, 2009; New Jersey Department of Children and Families; Office of Children and Family Services, New York State; American Society for the Positive Care of Children; Helpguide.org.

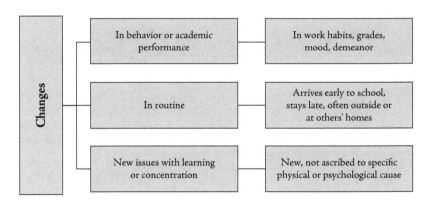

FIGURE 1.19   Changes

Source: Adapted from: USDHHS, Crosson-Tower, 2003; Children's Bureau, 2013; Prevent Child Abuse America, 2003; National Center for Child Traumatic Stress, 2009; New Jersey Department of Children and Families; Office of Children and Family Services, New York State; American Society for the Positive Care of Children; Helpguide.org.

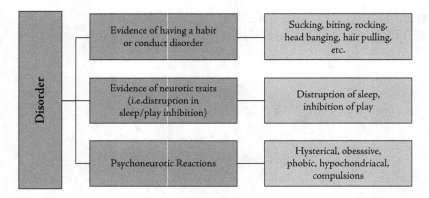

FIGURE 1.20   Disorder

Source: Adapted from: USDHHS, Crosson-Tower, 2003; Children's Bureau, 2013; Prevent Child Abuse America, 2003; National Center for Child Traumatic Stress, 2009; New Jersey Department of Children and Families; Office of Children and Family Services, New York State; American Society for the Positive Care of Children; Helpguide.org.

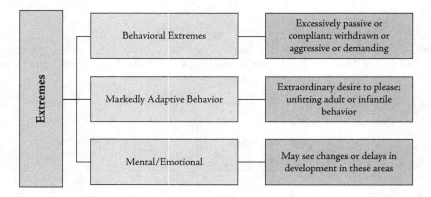

FIGURE 1.21   Extremes

Source: Adapted from: USDHHS, Crosson-Tower, 2003; Children's Bureau, 2013; Prevent Child Abuse America, 2003; National Center for Child Traumatic Stress, 2009; New Jersey Department of Children and Families; Office of Children and Family Services, New York State; American Society for the Positive Care of Children; Helpguide.org.

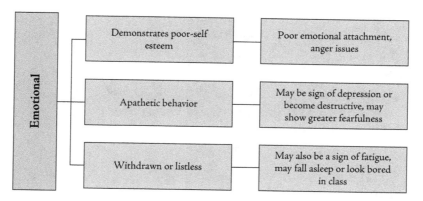

FIGURE 1.22   Emotional

Source: Adapted from: USDHHS, Crosson-Tower, 2003; Children's Bureau, 2013; Prevent Child Abuse America, 2003; National Center for Child Traumatic Stress, 2009; New Jersey Department of Children and Families; Office of Children and Family Services, New York State; American Society for the Positive Care of Children; Helpguide.org.

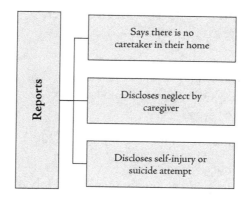

FIGURE 1.23   Reports

Source: Adapted from: USDHHS, Crosson-Tower, 2003; Children's Bureau, 2013; Prevent Child Abuse America, 2003; National Center for Child Traumatic Stress, 2009; New Jersey Department of Children and Families; Office of Children and Family Services, New York State; American Society for the Positive Care of Children; Helpguide.org.

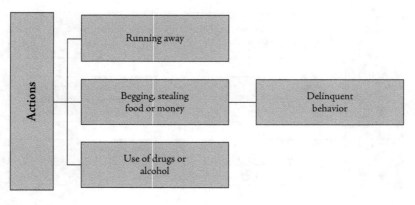

FIGURE 1.24   Actions

Source: Adapted from: USDHHS, Crosson-Tower, 2003; Children's Bureau, 2013; Prevent Child Abuse America, 2003; National Center for Child Traumatic Stress, 2009; New Jersey Department of Children and Families; Office of Children and Family Services, New York State; American Society for the Positive Care of Children; Helpguide.org.

Indicators or Warning Signs You Might Observe in the Parent or Caregiver

+ Lack of regard for or indifference to the child
+ Signs of depression or may appear apathetic
+ Behaves irrationally or in a bizarre manner
+ Abuse of alcohol or drugs

(childwelfare.gov, 2007, Prevent Child Abuse America, 2003)

+ Renounces the child's existence
+ Blames the child for problems at home and, or at school
+ Expects child to meet caregiver or parent's emotional or physical needs; looks to the child for care

(mayoclinic.org, n.d.)

Some Examples of Physical Child Neglect

1. Abandoning the child for long periods of time
2. Allowing the child to live in an unfit environment (e.g., bugs, rodents, feces, lack of plumbing, heat, or water)
3. Disregarding the child's need for medical care
4. Not providing food for the child
5. Not getting the child to school, or keeping the child home from school to care for the adult's needs
6. Not providing adequately for the child's clothing, such as sending them to school in subzero temperatures in a sweatshirt and sneakers

7. Not providing proper hygiene, such as bathing children, washing their hair, cleaning their clothes, or providing the means for older children to do so
8. Leaving a child in an unsafe place, such as a parked car

SEXUAL ABUSE

Nine-year-old Susan's mother works at night. Her stepfather James is around when she goes to bed, so many evenings James lies down beside Susan. As she goes to sleep, he rubs her breasts and genital area. (APA.org)

Child sexual abuse is frequently underreported and very hard to prove. As such, sexual abuse is sometimes called a hidden type of abuse. One out of three girls and one out of five boys will be sexually abused before they reach the age of 18 (dosomething.org: https://www. dosomething.org/us/facts/11-facts-about-child-abuse). Of all the types of abuse, sexual abuse is especially complex due to the guilt, shame and stigma attached to it. Stories of sexual predators and pedophiles are common and frightening. As a society, we do a fairly good job of educating our children about "stranger danger." Most children will learn in school about not taking rides with people they don't know, not helping strangers find lost puppies, and running away from scary looking people. However, the more terrifying truth is that sexual abuse usually occurs at the hands of someone the child knows and trusts, such as a family member or relative. In fact, 90% of child sexual abuse victims know the perpetrator in some manner; 68% are abused by a family member (dosomething.org). These are not the strangers about which we do such a fine job of warning children.

According to kidsmatterinc.org (n.d.) "Sexual abuse is any contact between a child and an adult for the adult's sexual stimulation" (para. 1). The American Society for the Protection of Cruelty to Children (americanspcc.org, n.d.) definition goes further, stating that "child sexual abuse is a type of maltreatment that refers to the involvement of the child in sexual activity to provide sexual gratification or financial benefit to the perpetrator, including contacts for sexual purposes, molestation, statutory rape, prostitution, pornography, exposure, incest, or other sexually exploitive activities" (p. 1). After reading these definitions carefully, it is clear that sexual exploitation can occur even if there is no bodily sexual contact. As noted by Babbel (2013, para.6), "It's important to notice this clause about 'no sexual contact.' Often, victims of sexual abuse will try to downplay their experience by saying that it 'wasn't that bad.' It's vital to recognize that abuse comes in many shapes, colors, and sizes and that all abuse is bad."

Regardless of the definition it is a very large and complicated issue, and it causes extreme damage to a child's health and well-being. Smith and Segal (2017) captured the problem extremely well in this statement:

> Aside from the physical damage that sexual abuse can cause, the emotional component is powerful and far reaching. Sexually abused children are tormented by shame and guilt. They may feel that they are responsible for the abuse or

somehow brought it upon themselves. This can lead to self-loathing and sexual problems as they grow older—often either excessive promiscuity or an inability to have intimate relations. (Sexual abuse, para.3)

To intensify the problem, the perpetrator in a child abuse scenario does not usually suddenly begin to molest a child. They frequently take time to "groom" the child.

> Grooming means in this context to gradually cross boundaries, setting the child up for victimization. It may start very innocently, just doing things with the child. Then the molester gradually does things closer and closer physically (e.g. sit next to the child, touch the child appropriately like shaking hands, putting a hand on a shoulder, an affectionate arm around the back, have the child sit on their lap, comb their hair, help put sunscreen on the child). The potential offender then begins to cross more of these "personal space boundaries." They may linger in these touches longer than appropriate, be more exuberant in showing affection, fingers seemingly accidentally touching more intimate parts, suggestions to be alone more and lying down with the child, wrestling or other activities which bring closer contact. (Family Learning Program, FIT.edu, n.d., Sexual Abuse-Red Flags)

During this grooming period, many red flags, justifications, and coercions are used. Berliner and Conte (1990) studied 23 victims of child sexual abuse and created a list of pre-abuse indicators reported by child victims. They included (to name only a few), being treated differently from other kids by the perpetrator, being told not to tell their mother the things they were doing together, saying they were special and the only one who understood, "accidentally" coming into bedroom or bathroom when the child was undressing, doing things that involved physical contact, giving special privileges, making the child feel obligated, and "teaching sex" with pornography or touching the child's body. Additionally, the researchers noted that perpetrators used justifications to get the child victim to be compliant and clandestine. These included such statements as: You like it, nobody will find out, you look older than you really are, I won't do it anymore, you are very mature for your age, you want me to do this, it makes me feel better, I'm teaching you about sex, I'm just going to play around; or as one child client of mine said to me, "what people don't understand is that some things are just fun and games … they're just fun and games." Another commonly used tactic was coercion. The authors noted threats of beating, telling the child that the mother would leave, that the family would be separated, that the abuser would kill himself, and that the family would be shamed. Indirect emotional coercion worked by telling the child that everyone would think they were a slut and that no one would like them. Many believe they deserved this; many blamed themselves.

It is such shame and guilt that make children reticent to come forward and disclose the sexual abuse. This is problematic, because unlike physical abuse, it is difficult to observe the physical signs of sexual abuse. Some children hide the physical signs well, and some show no signs at all. This makes it exceedingly difficult for the mandated reporters to suspect sexual abuse, which is a factor in its underreporting. Most often, it is behavioral or emotional signs that indicate sexual abuse.

Physical Indicators or Warning Signs of Sexual Abuse You Might Observe in the Child

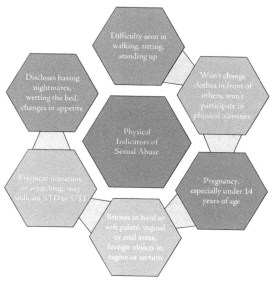

FIGURE 1.25   Physical Indicators or Warning Signs of Sexual Abuse You Might Observe in the Child

Source: Adapted from: USDHHS, Crosson-Tower, 2003; Children's Bureau, 2013; Prevent Child Abuse America, 2003; National Center for Child Traumatic Stress, 2009; New Jersey Department of Children and Families; Office of Children and Family Services, New York State; American Society for the Positive Care of Children; helpguide.org. Behavioral Indicators or Warning Signs of Sexual Abuse You Might Observe in the Child

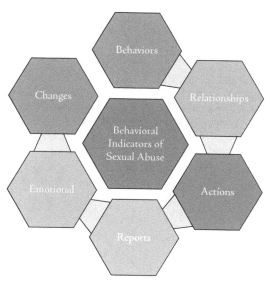

FIGURE 1.26   Behavioral Indicators or Warning Signs of Sexual Abuse You Might Observe in the Child

Source: Adapted from: USDHHS, Crosson-Tower, 2003; Children's Bureau, 2013; Prevent Child Abuse America, 2003; National Center for Child Traumatic Stress, 2009; New Jersey Department of Children and Families; Office of Children and Family Services, New York State; American Society for the Positive Care of Children; Helpguide.org.

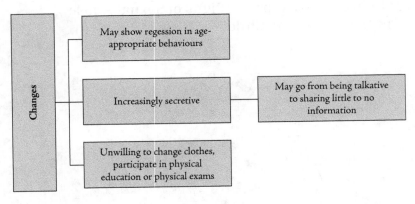

FIGURE 1.27   Changes

Source: Adapted from: USDHHS, Crosson-Tower, 2003; Children's Bureau, 2013; Prevent Child Abuse America, 2003; National Center for Child Traumatic Stress, 2009; New Jersey Department of Children and Families; Office of Children and Family Services, New York State; American Society for the Positive Care of Children; Helpguide.org.

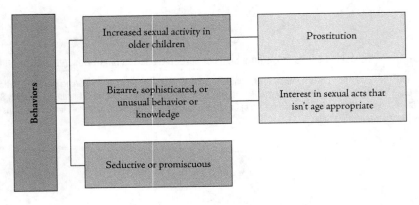

FIGURE 1.28   Behaviors

Source: Adapted from: USDHHS, Crosson-Tower, 2003; Children's Bureau, 2013; Prevent Child Abuse America, 2003; National Center for Child Traumatic Stress, 2009; New Jersey Department of Children and Families; Office of Children and Family Services, New York State; American Society for the Positive Care of Children; Helpguide.org.

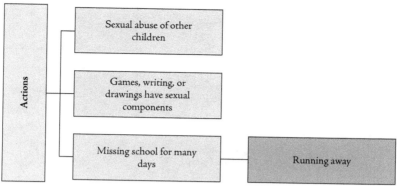

FIGURE 1.29   Actions

Source: Adapted from: USDHHS, Crosson-Tower, 2003; Children's Bureau, 2013; Prevent Child Abuse America, 2003; National Center for Child Traumatic Stress, 2009; New Jersey Department of Children and Families; Office of Children and Family Services, New York State; American Society for the Positive Care of Children; Helpguide.org.

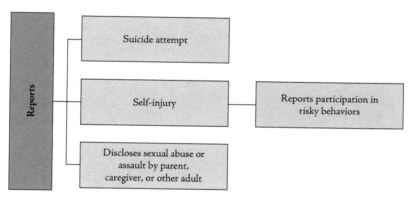

FIGURE 1.30   Reports

Source: Adapted from: USDHHS, Crosson-Tower, 2003; Children's Bureau, 2013; Prevent Child Abuse America, 2003; National Center for Child Traumatic Stress, 2009; New Jersey Department of Children and Families; Office of Children and Family Services, New York State; American Society for the Positive Care of Children; Helpguide.org.

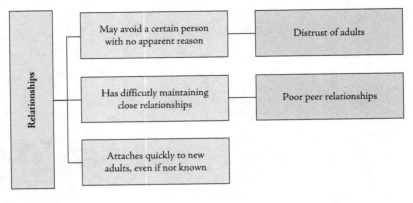

FIGURE 1.31   Relationships

Source: Adapted from: USDHHS, Crosson-Tower, 2003; Children's Bureau, 2013; Prevent Child Abuse America, 2003; National Center for Child Traumatic Stress, 2009; New Jersey Department of Children and Families; Office of Children and Family Services, New York State; American Society for the Positive Care of Children; Helpguide.org.

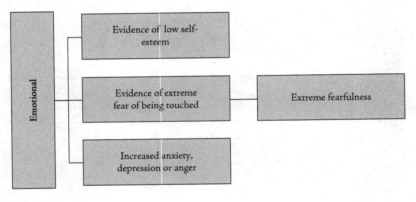

FIGURE 1.32   Emotional

Source: Adapted from: USDHHS, Crosson-Tower, 2003; Children's Bureau, 2013; Prevent Child Abuse America, 2003; National Center for Child Traumatic Stress, 2009; New Jersey Department of Children and Families; Office of Children and Family Services, New York State; American Society for the Positive Care of Children; Helpguide.org.

Indicators or Warning Signs You Might Observe in the Parent or Caregiver

+ Overly protective of the child
+ Isolates or sets strong limitations on who the child sees, where they go, and what they do
+ Adult may also be isolated, interacts little, or is very secretive
+ Adult may demonstrate jealousy of others, including family members
+ Adult may be controlling of child and other family members
+ May describe marital difficulties involving family power struggles or sexual relations

(Adapted from childwelfare.gov, 2007; Prevent Child Abuse America, 2003)

Some Examples of Sexual Abuse

1. Fondling a child's genitals
2. Having intercourse with a child
3. Having oral sex with a child
4. Having sex in front of a child
5. Having a child touch an older person's genitals
6. Using a child in pornography
7. Showing X-rated books or movies to a child

EMOTIONAL ABUSE AND NEGLECT

Dorrie's teacher found her test in the garbage can at the end of the day. Knowing that there would be a penalty if she didn't get it signed by a parent, the teacher approached Dorrie the next day. Dorrie said that the grade wasn't good enough. If she showed it to her mother, there would be endless interrogation ... "What was the highest grade? Were there bonus points? What was the highest grade you could have gotten? What did other people get?" These angry questions would be followed by a punishment; sometimes being grounded and studying extra hours for a week; and sometimes the loss of a personal possession (e.g., "my mother threw my I-Pod away"). Dorrie said she would rather take the penalty than take the test home to show it to her mother. Dorrie's grade on the test was 95.

Sticks and stones will break my bones, but words will never hurt me, right? I grew up hearing that, but nothing could be further from the truth. Many parents and caregivers feel that they are doing their jobs well because they never lay a hand on their children. However, the stark truth is that one can be abusive to children without touching them at all. Whether called emotional abuse or psychological maltreatment, it can be the most challenging type of abuse or maltreatment to prove. Some might say that most parents have been emotionally abusive to their children at some point or another. People lose their patience and say mean things when overtired and stressed. What, then, does this category of abuse and neglect entail?

Many definitions of this category exist, and you may hear it referred to as emotional abuse, emotional neglect, or even psychological maltreatment. As noted by Crosson-Tower (2005), it is common for this category to be divided in to two components: emotional/psychological abuse and emotional/psychological neglect. The division makes a clear contrast between two, wherein one is more active, and one is more passive. The use of threats of harm, emotional attacks, verbal assaults, and being held in confinement would be considered emotional abuse (e.g., the abuser is actively involved in harming the child). Emotional/psychological neglect is more passive, and includes insufficient nurturing and affection, refusal to provide suitable care, or knowingly allowing the child to take part in activities such as drug abuse or other possible criminal behaviors. However, these can seem like almost imperceptible distinctions because many of these factors coexist in abusive situations. It is also difficult to divorce emotional/psychological maltreatment from other types of abuse and neglect, as the two are often interwoven. Many who have experienced physical abuse have said that the emotional messages attached to the abuse ("you are a bad child," "you deserve to be punished," "this will teach you," "this is what happens to naughty children," etc.) leave scars that last long after the abuse is over. Sometimes physical abuse is followed by emotional abuse ("go to your room and stay there," or "keep crying and I'll give you something to cry about").

With so many gray areas, Crosson-Tower (2005) noted that a key to defining this type of abuse is determining that they are not isolated events, but patterns of behavior that may include the following:

- Rejecting—The caregiver does not acknowledge the child's worth or give value to their needs.
- Isolating—The caregiver isolates the child from social experiences and leads the child to believe that they are alone in the world.
- Terrorizing—The caregiver assaults the child verbally, thus creating a climate of fear and showing the world to be unsafe.
- Ignoring—The caregiver suppresses emotional growth and intellectual development by preventing the child from having appropriate stimulation.
- Corrupting—The caregiver, by encouraging engagement in destructive or antisocial behavior (or both), raises a child that cannot participate in normal social experiences.
- Destroying personal possessions
- Harming a pet

The messages sent by such treatment are reflected in a variety of behaviors. The example that comes to mind is the student who went from being the class leader to having the worst grades and behavior in the class as a result of his mother leaving his family. When asked why his behavior had changed so much, he answered that being a good kid wasn't enough to keep his mother home. Being bad was more fun so he might as well be bad. As a teacher, this was very hard to deal with, as he went from a solid student and role model to someone requiring constant supervision and redirection. His message was clear: "I don't care. I wasn't good enough for my mother, so I'm not going to try. Why bother." Another example was a child asked to write a sentence using the word *dad*. The child wrote about dad shooting his cat. This was followed by the question "Why?" ("Dad, why did you shoot my cat? I loved that cat.")

As mentioned above, emotional maltreatment can be divided into abuse and neglect. Emotional abuse can be as injurious to a child as physical abuse. The scars can be long-term and include emotional, behavioral, intellectual, and self-esteem damage. Emotional abuse can range from the absence of positive regard (such as lack of praise or encouragement), to harsh verbal assaults (such as screaming, threats, blaming, belittling, and cruel sarcasm).

Other conditions leading to emotional abuse can include negative parental moods, continuous family discord, and the communication of mixed messages (americanspcc.org).

> *Molly sat in my office coloring to get her mind off the oppressive feelings of sadness she had been experiencing lately. I reached into my desk and brought out my "magic wand" and handed it to her. "Molly, here's a magic wand. If it was real and you could get your mother to do ANYthing in the world, what would it be?" Molly rolled her eyes and glanced at me with a look that only a middle school girl could give. She looked at the wand, looked at me, and said wistfully, "Ask me how my day was".*

Emotional neglect (sometimes referred to as deprivation) can be described as "the deprivation suffered by children when their parents do not provide the normal experiences producing feelings of being loved, wanted, secure, and worthy" (americanspcc.org, 2018, emotional abuse section, para. 10.). Being ignored by caregivers can be as damaging as physical attacks for some children. Very young children, especially, are very needy of warmth, affection, positive touch, smiles, and other caring interactions. Children who do not receive this kind of attention might even go as far as exhibiting negative behavior resulting in abuse, rather than having no interaction at all.

Emotional abuse or neglect is frequently seen as the foundational issue behind the majority of what damages a child, regardless of the type of abuse being reported. As will be discussed in a later section, emotional abuse and neglect are extremely hard to prove. The American Society for the Prevention of Cruelty to Children (SPCC) noted that "… reporting these situations is not mandated unless they constitute a form of legally defined abuse or neglect"(americanspcc.org, 2018, emotional abuse section para. 13). Despite the difficulty in defining and reporting this, it remains a key problem for children's mental and emotional well-being and cannot be discounted. Never forget that you have the power to give positive messages to children and adolescents in your work and daily interactions with them. While this will not make up for the deficits caused by the emotional maltreatment by their parents, it can help them to see themselves in a more positive light, thus providing a much-needed boost to their lagging self-esteem.

Indicators or Warning Signs of Emotional Abuse
You Might Observe in the Child

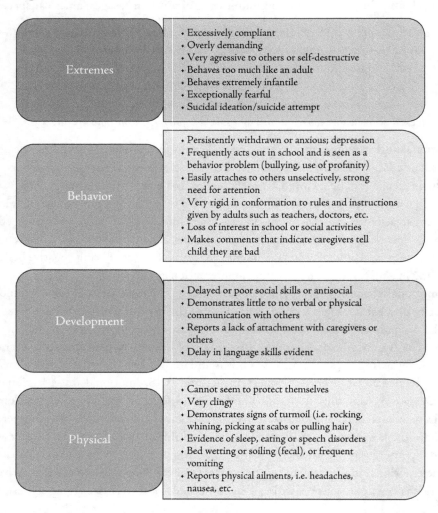

Extremes
- Excessively compliant
- Overly demanding
- Very aggressive to others or self-destructive
- Behaves too much like an adult
- Behaves extremely infantile
- Exceptionally fearful
- Sucidal ideation/suicide attempt

Behavior
- Persistently withdrawn or anxious; depression
- Frequently acts out in school and is seen as a behavior problem (bullying, use of profanity)
- Easily attaches to others unselectively, strong need for attention
- Very rigid in conformation to rules and instructions given by adults such as teachers, doctors, etc.
- Loss of interest in school or social activities
- Makes comments that indicate caregivers tell child they are bad

Development
- Delayed or poor social skills or antisocial
- Demonstrates little to no verbal or physical communication with others
- Reports a lack of attachment with caregivers or others
- Delay in language skills evident

Physical
- Cannot seem to protect themselves
- Very clingy
- Demonstrates signs of turmoil (i.e. rocking, whining, picking at scabs or pulling hair)
- Evidence of sleep, eating or speech disorders
- Bed wetting or soiling (fecal), or frequent vomiting
- Reports physical ailments, i.e. headaches, nausea, etc.

FIGURE 1.33   Indicators or Warning Signs of Emotional Abuse That Can be Observed in the Child

Source: Adapted from: "Emotional Child Abuse," americanspcc.org. American Society for the Positive Care of Children and "Signs and Symptoms of Child Abuse," ky.gov. Commonwealth of Kentucky.

Indicators or Warning Signs of Emotional Neglect or Deprivation You Might Observe in the Child

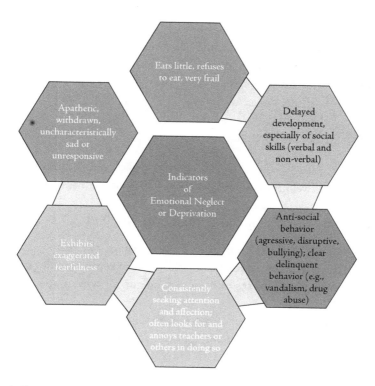

FIGURE 1.34 Indicators or Warning Signs of Emotional Neglect or Deprivation That Can be Observed in the Child

Source: Adapted from: "Emotional Child Abuse," americanspcc.org. American Society for the Positive Care of Children.

As always, these behavior patterns could be due to other causes. It is important, though, to be aware that the suspicion of emotional abuse or neglect should not be dismissed.

Indicators or Warning Signs You Might Observe in the Parent or Care Giver

+ Extremely harsh, negative, or critical of the child to others or in public
+ Name calling, blaming, berating, or belittling the child (may call the child "it" or "thing")
+ Blatantly rejects the child
+ Uses the child to fulfill their own needs; child is too young or immature to understand
+ Ascribes fault to the child consistently
+ Holds unrealistic and unreasonable expectations of the child
+ Demonstrates lack of concern for the child

- Refuses offers of help for the child's problems
- Involves the child in overly adult situations (e.g., uses marital conflicts as a battle ground)
- Admits to not liking the child or hating the child
- Attempts to interfere with the child's relationship with another parent or caretaker
- Withdraws comfort as a method of discipline
- Appears cold or unsupportive
- Suffers from drug or alcohol abuse
- Threatens the child with severe punishments
- Appears to have a violent nature

(americanspcc.org, 2018; Prevent Child Abuse America, n.d.; education.ky.gov, CHFS training, 2016; childwelfare.gov, 2007; Prevent Child Abuse America, 2003)

Some Examples of Emotional Abuse and Neglect

- Continually humiliating, shaming, or demeaning the child
- Calling the child names; comparing the child to something negative
- Consistently using phrases like "you are no good," "what a mistake you were," or "you are a bad child"
- Repeatedly threatening, yelling at, or bullying the child
- Using rejection as a punishment; ignoring the child; use of silent treatment
- Having little physical contact with the child; depriving the child of physical affection (e.g., hugs)
- Exposing the child to violence toward others, another parent or child, or a pet or other animal
- Destroying or throwing away the child's toys, clothing, or other possessions

(Smith, Robinson, Saisan & Segal, 2017 in Helpguide.org)

COMMON MYTHS AND FACTS ABOUT CHILD ABUSE AND NEGLECT

MYTH vs. TRUTH
(National Child Traumatic Stress Network [NCTSN] Child Physical Abuse Fact Sheet, 2009; Smith, Robinson, Saisan & Segal, 2017 in HelpGuide.org)

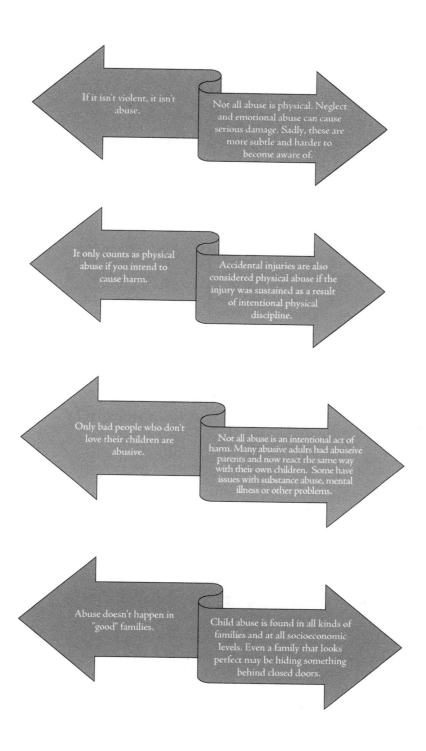

If it isn't violent, it isn't abuse.

Not all abuse is physical. Neglect and emotional abuse can cause serious damage. Sadly, these are more subtle and harder to become aware of.

It only counts as physical abuse if you intend to cause harm.

Accidental injuries are also considered physical abuse if the injury was sustained as a result of intentional physical discipline.

Only bad people who don't love their children are abusive.

Not all abuse is an intentional act of harm. Many abusive adults had abuseive parents and now react the same way with their own children. Some have issues with substance abuse, mental illness or other problems.

Abuse doesn't happen in "good" families.

Child abuse is found in all kinds of families and at all socioeconomic levels. Even a family that looks perfect may be hiding something behind closed doors.

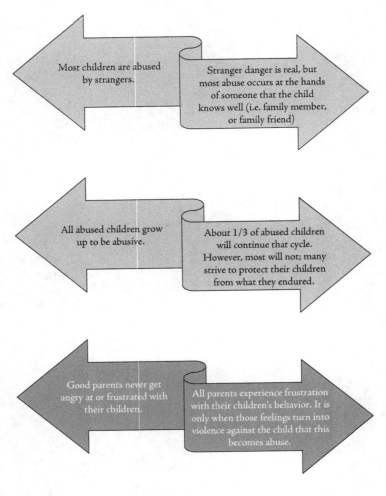

FIGURE 1.35   Myth vs. Truth

Source: Adapted from: "Child Physical Abuse Fact Sheet," nctsn.org. National Center for Child Traumatic Stress, 2009.

PUNISHMENT VERSUS ABUSE

As a toddler, Ethan was hard to control. When they attempted to control him, his parents would give him a swat on the hand or thigh. When Ethan began preschool his teacher informed the parents that he was disruptive in the classroom. When this happened, his parents spanked him as punishment. In kindergarten Ethan began to get into fights with other students. His father wanted to deal with this harshly, by whipping him with his belt, and Mom agreed with this approach. She had been spanked, sometimes with a belt, and she had turned out just fine. By the time Ethan was in second grade, he was fighting not only in school, but also at home and around the neighborhood. One day his parents found out that Ethan had lied to them about getting into trouble at school again. His father intended to spank Ethan, but instead hit him across the mouth as punishment for lying. When the child began talking back to his father, he was hit on his back and buttocks. Ethan didn't stop talking back and his father hit him harder and harder. When it ended, the child was crying to the point of not being able to speak or breathe easily. (adapted from NCTSN, 2009)

As a mandated child abuse reporting instructor, people ask me questions all the time. One of the most frequent questions or comments I receive has to do with physical punishment. "Do you mean to tell me, I can't spank my kid?" Other comments I have heard over the years include "I was spanked, and I turned out just fine;" "I think what's wrong with the world today is that parents are afraid to spank their kids"; "If my kids talked to me that way, they'd get the back of my hand," to name a few. What results is usually a heated and contentious debate between those who think physical punishment is the key to raising good children and those who believe that it is just another form of abuse. The truth is that there is sometimes a fine line between what is seen as discipline and what could be defined as abuse. Many states delineate between acceptable corporal punishment (such as spanking a child on the bottom a couple of times for running out into the street) and what is considered abusive (such as beating a child with a belt or stick and leaving bruises). This varies among states, with some having much stricter laws against physical punishment than others.

Parents might agree that the management of children's behavior poses one of the biggest challenges to raising them. Many parents see physical punishment as an acceptable means of doing this. Over two-thirds of American adults agreed that children sometimes need "a good hard spanking" (National Opinion Research Center, 2006). While physical punishment may be seen as the best (or perhaps the only) way to handle a child's problematic behavior, there is research that indicates that there are better methods of discipline. "Spanking may work temporarily to stop children's problem behaviors, but it may not change their behavior in the long run" (NCTSN, 2009). Physical punishment can also escalate in severity and lead to abuse. As children grow, what might have worked in the past (a swat on the butt) can prove to be ineffective with an older child. This could result in additional force, duration, or the use of an implement to get the desired effect, thus crossing the line into abuse.

On top of the physical pain, corporal punishment causes emotional distress in children and can harm the relationship between children and their parents. Many emotions are associated with the punishment: anger, fear, guilt, helplessness, shame, powerlessness, and others. The affects may be far reaching, causing children to be fearful and closed off from discussing feelings and problems. Or children may learn from this that physical force is the answer to contention, leading them to be more aggressive themselves. The old adage "this is going to hurt me more than it will hurt you," spoken by the caregiver, is far from true. Children depend on love, care, and support from their parents and caregivers. When the people they are supposed to trust and rely upon the most hurt them, it is confusing for them to say the least. This can lead to damage to a child's sense of self, and can even effect emotional and mental development, as well as school performance (Gershoff, 2008).

While it is not mandated to report physical punishment unless it crosses that line into being abusive, you may have the opportunity to help a parent or caregiver find another way of disciplining their child. I have been asked in the past "well, if I can't hit them with the stick, how am I supposed to control them?" In the resources section of this book you will find several places to look for information on more effective forms of discipline. If you are afforded the opportunity to do so, you may wish to share some of this information with parents. If you have a monthly newsletter, perhaps a piece on positive discipline would be an appropriate addition from time to time. You never know what effect it might have on a stressed out and overwhelmed parent reading it. Many caregivers know no other way to discipline and any new information might help a child in the long run.

CHILD ABUSE AND MALTREATMENT OF CHILDREN WITH DISABILITIES

Child abuse is a problem in America affecting children of all backgrounds and abilities. However, children with disabilities are at a greater risk (Orelove, Hollahan, & Myles, 2000). According to the Child Welfare Information Gateway (2012), "children with disabilities were 1.5 times more likely to be seriously harmed by the abuse or neglect they experienced" (Sedlak et al, 2010, p.3). It was also noted that one study found that children with a behavioral health condition were at risk for continued abuse, and several studies indicated that emotional or behavioral disorders present the greatest risk to children.

Societal attitudes may play a huge role in placing children with disabilities at higher risk for abuse and neglect. According to Steinberg and Hylton (1998), by devaluing children with disabilities and their societal contributions, it can become more acceptable to use violence against them or otherwise treat them poorly. The authors also noted that there are many myths regarding children with disabilities which can perpetuate maltreatment, such as the belief that some children with disabilities do not feel pain, cannot manage their behavior themselves, are asexual. Additionally, Sobsey (1994) reported that when disabled children are separated from their peers, it can lead to them seeing themselves as different and perhaps unworthy of the same opportunities as others, both socially and educationally. Another point of which to be aware is that children with disabilities may feel shame or less worthy of being treated well or may not be aware of proper treatment or what to do if they are maltreated (National Resource Center on Child Sex Abuse, 1994). It is disheartening that such factors in society may lend themselves to the perpetuation of abuse in children with special needs. In a world where it is vital for professionals to have appropriate training in identifying and reporting suspected child maltreatment, there appears to be a lack of training in this area for those who work with exceptional children. The nature of some children's disabilities could very well prevent them from protecting themselves or reporting abuse to another caregiver. Thus, it is vastly important that all professionals who work with disabled children be highly trained in these topics (childwelfare.gov, 2001, 2012).

In addition to societal risk factors, risk factors are also present in the families and the children themselves. Some of these include a family that views the child as abnormal and an embarrassment, the lack of skills to care for a child with disabilities, and the financial strain of caring for a child and its resultant stress. Children whose disabilities present challenging behaviors or who have intensive needs may be overwhelming to caregivers, thus exacerbating the problem (Child Information Gateway, 2012).

Anything done to isolate and dehumanize children with disabilities, including in schools and classrooms, only serves to give power to this issue. As stated by the Child Welfare Information Gateway (2012), awareness of the problem is the first step to dealing with it. After that, there are several strategies put forth by the organization to help change attitudes regarding children with disabilities in schools and in society.

- **Educate community members to the higher risk factors associated with being disabled.** People may not know that exceptional children have a higher risk of being maltreated, nor how to best provide them with increased supports and protections.
- **Assist others in seeing children with special needs as "valued and unique individuals"** (p. 9). This can be done by pointing out the children's strengths and unique gifts and viewpoints to others, including faculty, family, and students.
- **"Promote inclusion of children with disabilities in everyday life"** (p. 9).
- **Foster communities to take part in sharing the responsibility for the safety and overall welfare of children with disabilities.** Help to strengthen parent-child interactions by teaching parents communication techniques and supporting positive interactions with children (p. 9).

Finally, always work with the children to help them to understand and protect themselves to the best of their abilities. Some suggestions include teaching children about their and others' bodies and safety, reducing social isolation of children with disabilities, involving parents in their children's education, and maximizing children's communication skills and tools by practicing with them and modeling healthy interactions (Child Information Gateway, 2012). Information and communication among all parties is the key to greater safety for children with disabilities. As noted by Orelove, Hollahan & Myles (2000), "Equipping central players in the maltreatment arena with disability-specific knowledge has historically been a missing element in the design of response systems to abuse and neglect of children with special needs" (p. 194). Education professionals are in a strong position to assist in this process by receiving training, and thus, helping to make life safer for children with disabilities.

DOMESTIC VIOLENCE

Domestic violence can be defined as a behavioral pattern used by one adult in a household to create a situation in which that adult has power and control over the other. The tools of choice are often fear and intimidation, including the use of violence or the threat thereof (safehorizon.org). By some estimates, over three million children witness domestic violence in their homes each year (childwitnesstoviolence.org, n.d.). This is a huge and far-reaching problem in society today. I am frequently asked if domestic violence is child abuse. While domestic violence is not, by itself, inherently a category of child abuse, there is a very strong correspondence between the two. Children who live in households where domestic violence is present can suffer abuse at much higher rates; these are noted as high as 30% to 60% depending on the study (childwitnesstoviolence.org). Children who try to intervene in a violent dispute between their parents often get injured as a result; the child becomes collateral damage in the situation. In some circumstances this has led to the death of the intervening child. Even if there is no physical damage, children can be emotionally scarred by being a witness to domestic violence. Despite the lack of its definition as a category of abuse, it is important for professionals to have an understanding of the warning signs and effects of domestic violence. Any child that you suspect is living in a violent household bears watching carefully. Many resources are available to assist adults who are dealing with this problem. Sometimes this support and information can come from teachers, school counselors, or mental health care workers that have the opportunity to provide it.

Warning Signs of Domestic Violence in Adults and or Children

As stated by Kids Matter, Inc. (2016):
   "Warning signs of domestic violence include the following:

   + Frequent injuries, with the excuse of 'accidents'
   + Frequent and sudden absences from work or school
   + Child is afraid of inviting another child to his/her home
   + Personality changes in a parent (e.g., an outgoing woman becomes withdrawn)
   + Excessive fear of conflict
   + Submissive behavior, lack of assertiveness
   + Isolation from friends and family
   + Depression, crying, low self-esteem"

(kidsmatterinc.org/get-help/for-families/abuse-and-neglect/children-domestic-violence/, para. 3)

Some Effects of Exposure to Violence on Children

The Child Witness to Violence Project (www.childwitnesstoviolence.org, n.d.) indicated these common symptoms that may be observed in children who have been a witness to violence:

   + **Sleep problems**—fear of falling asleep, waking up frequently, bad dreams

- **Physical Complaints**—stomach aches, headaches, or other aches and pains that have no apparent medical cause; may also be lethargic or fatigued (safehorizon.org)
- **An increase in aggressive behavior or outbursts of anger**—child may engage in fights, or fight more often
- **More active than usual**
- **Hypervigilance**—(also a symptom of Post-traumatic stress disorder [PTSD]) may show increased amounts of anxiety, worry, or fear, or have an "overreaction to loud noises or sudden movements" (para. 5)
- **Signs of Regression**—losing skills already learned or adopting infantile behavior (e.g., wetting their pants again, thumb sucking, etc.)
- **Withdrawal**—demonstrates a lack of interest in social or academic activities and people once important to the child or enjoyable
- **Numbing**—expresses no feelings or concerns; not troubled by anything
- **Increase in Separation Anxiety**—refusal to go to school, transitions are upsetting, demonstrates anxiety when left with a childcare person
- **Easily Distracted**—inability to learn, unable to focus or concentrate at home, socially, or at school
- **Changes in Play**—child acts out or repeats recreations of violent events through play; less creative and spontaneous play
- **Natural Curiosity Impeded**—basic drive to explore the world may be hindered; less likely to try new things
- **Higher Risk**—may be at higher risk of becoming violent or having adjustment problems
- **PTSD may be evident**—exhibits symptoms found in post-traumatic stress disorder

(http://www.childwitnesstoviolence.org/symptoms-of-witnessing-violence.html)

POST-TRAUMATIC STRESS DISORDER IN CHILDREN

One girl's classroom experience:

The room began to peak with noise as chairs gave a metallic screech on the floor, chattering about last night's dance and obnoxiously loud laughter. My teacher clapped her hands to draw the attention of my class which made me grit my teeth in pain. My head was beginning to spin, and I could feel my breath get caught between my lungs and my ribs. I felt a collection of cold sweat gather in a film across my face. I trembled as the images caught across my vision. I was crouched down behind my bedroom door as my father stood above me with his hand raise ready to slap me. My mouth went dry and a shot of fear coursed through my veins. I blinked my eyes a few times and reminded myself that I was safe. Yet, I felt alert and anxious for the rest of class.

~ Survivor of abuse (personal communication, 2016)

Once thought of as found only in combat veterans, Post-Traumatic Stress Disorder (PTSD) can also result from being raised in violent situations; because of this, children can exhibit signs of PTSD. PTSD is a psychological disorder that can develop in anyone who has been exposed to danger or was harmed in some way. They may not have been able to protect themselves in the situation. Under these circumstances, a child experiences fear, powerlessness, and helplessness, which can make PTSD more likely (asca.org.au). Since child abuse and domestic violence put children in unpredictable, fear producing, and helpless situations, they are viewed as traumatic events.

As stated previously, adverse childhood experiences can actually cause changes in children's brains that have far-reaching and enduring effects. In a study on this subject, Anda, Felitti, Bremner, Walker, Whitfield, Perry, Cube and Giles (2006) wrote: "Childhood maltreatment has been linked to a variety of changes in brain structure and function and stress-responsive neurobiological systems" (p. 174). The authors noted that epidemiological studies have documented the impact of childhood trauma on the brain. The human brain depends on a variety of remarkable factors, each influencing the brain's development and expression of that which was inherited (the genome). As stated by Anda, et. al (2006)

> Unfortunately, this elegant sequence is vulnerable to extreme, repetitive, or abnormal patterns of stress during critical or circumscribed periods of childhood brain development that can impair, often permanently, the activity of major neuroregulatory systems, with profound and lasting neurobehavioral consequences. (p.174)

They go on to add, "An expanding body of evidence … suggests that early stressors cause long term changes in multiple brain circuits and systems" (p. 175). These changes can have negative effects on both social attachment and regulation of mood. Due to the variety of serious stressors in some children's lives, adverse early childhood experiences can lead to PTSD in some populations of abuse survivors. Some of these children may have cognitive problems as well. The authors also noted that "early abuse and PTSD is associated with increased cortisol and norepinephrine levels in children … and increased stress-induced cortisol responses" (p. 175). They sum this up well:

> Thus, childhood abuse and exposure to domestic violence can lead to numerous differences in the structure and physiology of the brain that expectedly would affect multiple human functions and behaviors. (p. 75)

With information from the world of neuroscience as a backdrop, we can more easily see how children could be changed by early experiences of violence or maltreatment. The causes of PTSD in children, then, are founded in neurobiology due to repeated exposure to stress tempered by genetics. On the list of traumatic events which could cause PTSD are sexual abuse, physical abuse, childhood neglect, and witnessing domestic violence (Anda, et. al, 2006; helpguide.org, n.d.). Because of this, at least some knowledge of the symptoms would be beneficial for teachers and counselors working with children and adolescents.

The symptoms of PTSD in children can be different from those found in adults, but common to all cases are the three main symptoms:

1. Hyperarousal
2. Re-experiencing (also called intrusion)
3. Avoidance

Hyperarousal

Have you ever had way too much caffeine? It can make you jumpy and easily startled. This is what hyperarousal is like. According to Dorland's Medical Dictionary, hyperarousal is "a state of increased psychological and physiological tension marked by such effects as reduced pain tolerance, anxiety, exaggeration of startle responses, insomnia, fatigue and accentuation of personality traits" (2007, as cited in Bailey, E., 2013, para.1). Also known as the "fight or flight" response, hyperarousal is part of what kept early man alive. Constant threats from the elements, wild animals, and the search for food often necessitated the surge of cortisol that gave them the burst of alertness and energy needed to deal with the situation by fighting or running away. Physiologically, when this occurs you experience a rapid heartbeat, shallow breathing, you are very alert, and your muscles tense (healthcentral.com). This serves us well in perilous situations. However, in the modern world, we frequently find ourselves in this condition for not only physical, but emotional reasons as well. This can be our response to avoiding a car accident or having to speak in front of a large group of people. Some people live their lives in chronic states of fight or flight. This is particularly true of children in abusive and violent households who feel threatened every day. The longer this response remains active, the more physically and emotionally draining it becomes (healthcentral.com). As someone working with children, this can be a difficult trait to witness. If you feel that a child with whom you work is frequently jumpy, overly nervous, or overreacts to sounds and situations, this is something to which you should pay attention.

Re-experiencing (Intrusion)

When a person goes through a traumatic experience, replaying the situation mentally is fairly common. Someone who has had an accident might say "I keep seeing the accident when I close my eyes." This sense of reliving the trauma is called re-experiencing, or intrusion. Survivors of trauma frequently relive those events, which can occur in various ways, but most involve having a memory which returns when not expected, or which is triggered by something (such as a sound, smell, or situation). According to Magellan Health Services (2001, adapted from Carlson and Ruzek),

> Re-experiencing means that the survivor continues to have the same mental, emotional, and physical experiences that occurred during or just after the trauma. This includes thinking about the trauma, seeing images of the event, feeling agitated, and having physical sensations like those that occurred during

the trauma. Trauma survivors find themselves feeling and acting as if the trauma is happening again: feeling as if they are in danger, experiencing panic sensations, wanting to escape, getting angry, thinking about attacking or harming someone else. (para. 3)

When working with children, a teacher or counselor might see this present itself in many ways. Intrusion can manifest itself as children or adolescents who seem to be constantly looking for danger or ways in which things could go wrong, who are easily startled, overly fearful, aggressive, or self-defensive (Magellan Health Services, 2001, adapted from Carson and Ruzek). Additionally, you may see a completely unexpected reaction to something. A student with whom I work recently told me of a time when a teacher tried to hug her. The angle of the teacher's arm in relationship to the student's body was a trigger, bringing her back to a time when her father was wielding a butcher knife. Her reaction was to jump backward to stay safe. The teacher was, obviously, confused (and perhaps hurt) by this. If a reaction makes no sense to you, this is, again, a reason to pay attention.

Avoidance

Thinking about the traumatic event is extremely upsetting for the survivor. Intrusions or flashbacks of the event are equally disturbing. Because these are so very unsettling, individuals with PTSD may strive to avoid any reminders or triggers of the traumatic event. An example not related to child abuse would be a child who lived through a bad flood not wanting it to rain. To steer clear of thinking about the event, survivors may avoid many possible triggers, such as conversations, places, activities, TV shows, movies, watching the news, or situations that might present a danger (Nebraska Department of Veterans Affairs, http://www.ptsd.ne.gov/what-is-ptsd.html). Another part of avoidance is referred to as *numbing*. This is another way to avoid the event by pushing down feelings, trying to be emotionally numb, isolating oneself from others, or not engaging in previously enjoyed activities (http://www.ptsd.ne.gov/what-is-ptsd.html). Survivors of trauma involved in avoidance often report feeling strange, or unlike themselves, or as if they have shut down emotionally. They may also have trouble with positive emotions, such as love (Magellan Health Services, 2001, adapted from Carlson & Ruzek). Again, this may be hard to see in your work with children and adolescents, but it is something to watch for with trauma survivors.

Symptoms of PTSD in Children and Adolescents

The symptoms of Post-Traumatic Stress Disorder in children can be different from those experienced by adults. This is especially true in very young children. Helpguide.org provides an excellent list of possible symptoms of which to be aware (Smith, Robinson & Segal, 2017, in helpguide.org, PTSD Symptoms in Children):

- "Fear of being separated from parent
- Losing previously-acquired skills (such as toilet training)

- Sleep problems and nightmares
- Somber, compulsive play in which themes or aspects of the trauma are repeated
- New phobias and anxieties that seem unrelated to the trauma (such as fear of monsters)
- Increase in aggression or irritability
- Difficulty concentrating
- Acting out the trauma through play, stories or drawings" (para. 13).

(https://helpguide.org/articles/ptsd-trauma/ptsd-symptoms-self-help-treatment.htm, para.13)

PTSD presents differently in children than it does in adults (PTSD in adolescents more closely mimics adult symptoms). Because of this, it would be beneficial to pay attention to not only the points mentioned above, but also to persistent negative thinking, changes in mood or extreme negative moods, and anxiety. Negative thinking may include self-blame, increased feelings of anger, shame, fear, and guilt, and constant worries about the world being an unsafe place in which to be (kidshealth.org). If you see evidence of PTSD symptoms, it is advised to consult a mental health professional about further diagnosis and treatment for the child. However, if you think there is an active abuse situation going on in the home, the correct course of action is to report this suspicion first.

CONSEQUENCES OF CHILD ABUSE AND NEGLECT

In light of the vast numbers (both reported and potentially unreported) of maltreated children today, we can only see the tip of the proverbial iceberg that is the legacy of child abuse and neglect. The mechanics of assessment and reporting of child abuse and neglect are only part of the overall problem. The effects of child abuse and neglect have consequences on children far beyond their school years and, often, throughout their entire lives. Adult lives have taken sad turns as a result of their childhood abuse. About 14% of men and 36% of women in prison in the United States were abused as children, which is about twice the frequency of that found in the general population. Children who were victims of abuse and neglect are approximately nine times more likely to be involved in criminal activity (americanspcc.org, n.d.). Other startling statistics include the following:

- Children who have been abused are 25% more likely to become pregnant as teenagers than those who have not been abused (Snyder, 2000, cited in americanspcc.org).
- Adolescents who have been abused during their lives are more prone to early sexual behavior and taking sexual risks, which can put them in greater danger of getting STD's (Snyder, 2000, cited in americanspcc.org).
- Approximately one-third of adults who experienced childhood abuse or neglect go on to be abusive to their offspring (www.childwelfare.gov, 2013).

- In at least one study, about 80% of 21-year-olds that had experienced abuse as children met the current criteria for one or more mental health conditions (Silverman, Reinhertz & Giaconia, 1996 cited in americanspcc.org).
- As many as 80% of those being treated for substance abuse reported that they had been abused or neglected as children (nccafv.org, n.d.).
- Adolescents who have reported being abused or neglected are three times more likely than those who did not report abuse to have a substance use issue before age 18 years (childwelfare.gov, 2003).
- Children who experienced abuse or neglect are about nine times more likely than children who didn't to become involved in some form of criminal behavior at some point (Snyder, 2000, cited in americanspcc.org).
- People who reported having been abused as children are at greater risk of committing a crime and going to prison than those who did not (Snyder, 2000, cited in americanspcc.org).
- The estimated annual cost of child abuse and neglect in America is $585 billion dollars (Fang, 2012, cited in americanspcc.org).

The Centers for Disease Control and Prevention conducted a study (The CDC-Kaiser ACE Study) on the exposure of children to adverse experiences such as abuse, neglect, or other traumatic stressors. Their findings indicated that an increase in adverse childhood experiences leads to a heightened risk for the following health problems (cdc.org, n.d. About the CDC-Kaiser ACE Study, Major Findings Section):

- Alcoholism and alcohol abuse
- Chronic obstructive pulmonary disease
- Depression
- Fetal death
- Health-related quality of life
- Illicit drug use
- Ischemic heart disease
- Liver disease
- Risk for intimate partner violence
- Multiple sexual partners
- Sexually transmitted diseases
- Smoking
- Suicide attempts
- Unintended pregnancies
- Early initiation of smoking
- Early initiation of sexual activity
- Adolescent Pregnancy

Health problems, drug abuse, sexual risk taking, criminal activity … the scars of child abuse and neglect are many. Some may be physical, but others are emotional and can cause damage to a child's sense of self, school performance, ability to create and sustain healthy relationships, and even ability to function in all areas. If you look at the above statistics, you can almost see an invisible thread leading back to the damage done to a child's development as a result of the abuse and neglect. The Joyful Heart Foundation puts it quite well:

> The brain develops at an incredible pace during the early developmental stages of infancy and childhood. Studies about early childhood development indicate that the brain develops in response to experiences with caregivers, family and community, and that its development is directly linked to the quality and quantity of those experiences. Meeting a child's needs during these early stages creates emotional stability and security that is needed for healthy brain development. Repeated exposure to stressful events can affect the brain's stress response, making it more reactive and less adaptive … children exposed to violence or abuse, if left unaddressed or ignored, are at an increased risk for emotional and behavioral problems in the future. (joyfulheartfoundation.org, n.d., Developmental and psychological effects, para. 1)

There have also been numerous studies that have used MRI technology to study the brains of children who have been abused and then to compare them to children who have not experienced such levels of fear or violence. These studies have shown that vital regions of the brain can fail to grow properly as a result of the maltreatment. This impaired development may have significant effects on cognitive, language, and academic abilities and may also have connections to various mental health disorders (Child Welfare Information Gateway; Tarullo, 2012). Continual stress and fear can also create other problems in an abused child's brain. For example, some children develop a persistent fear state. While this state was self-protective during the episodes of threat, it is counterproductive during other times when danger is not present. This can lead to hypervigilance, anxiety, and greater impulsivity (Perry, 2012, cited in Child Welfare Information Gateway). Such characteristics could be, then, perceived by caregivers *as difficult* and responses to them might be harsher, leading to the creation of a cycle. Glaser (2000) noted that these children are "doubly vulnerable, first to their own inherent responses to stress, and second, when they are met with insensitive and punitive caregiving responses which will be perceived by the infant or child as stressful" (p. 103). As a result of impairments to healthy brain development stemming from child maltreatment, there is an increased likelihood of the development of many mental health problems including, anxiety, depression, dissociation, flashbacks, difficulty sleeping, difficulty regulating emotions, problems connecting with others and creating relationships, increased hypervigilance, difficulty sleeping, self-harm, eating disorders, discomfort with physical touch, and even symptoms of PTSD (joyful-heartfoundation.org, n.d.; Child Welfare Information Gateway, 2008).

If you think back to your child development class, Erik Erikson (1959) noted the first stage of psychosocial development to be trust vs. mistrust. According to McLeod (2018), during an infant's first year of life, there is much uncertainty about the world around them. "To resolve these feelings of uncertainty, the infant looks towards their primary caregiver for stability and consistency of care" (p. 2). Smith and Segal (2013) put this quite succinctly: "If you can't trust your parents, who can you trust? Abuse by a primary caregiver damages the most fundamental relationship as a child—that you will safely, reliably get your physical and emotional needs met by the person who is responsible for your care. Without this base, it is very difficult to learn to trust people or know who is trustworthy" (p. 2).

A child who experiences mistrust can have difficulty with future relationships. They may also have trouble with emotional regulation because of trying to keep their feelings and emotions stuffed down due to fear of further abuse. This can result in these emotions coming to the surface unexpectedly and in a variety of ways including anger, anxiety, and depression (Smith and Segal, 2013).

Finally, at the heart of the abused child is a feeling of worthlessness. Many abused children have heard repeated messages that they are ugly, stupid, fat, worthless, unloved, unwanted, and bad, over, and over, and over again. These messages coming from one's primary caregivers are powerful and can damage core feelings of self-worth and self-esteem. Now add possible abuse or neglect on top of that. The message, then, is not only that the child is worthless, but they are so bad that they deserve to be hurt or ignored. These feelings of inadequacy can continue for a lifetime. The damage done to the child's self-worth may manifest itself in their adult life in numerous ways, such as lack of effort to accomplish goals, having trouble with success, and not feeling worthy of good things, to name a few. This can prevent them from getting better jobs, more education, or having better relationships because they feel that don't deserve it. Some may turn to alcohol or drugs to numb the pain. Some get caught in abusive relationships that reinforce the message that they deserve to be hurt. The consequences of child abuse and neglect are, indeed, numerous and can affect a person's emotional, social, cognitive, and mental well-being long after the abuse has ended.

It must be mentioned that with regard to the above section, again, this is not true for all. Having experienced abuse or neglect as a child does not doom the child to a horrible life. The consequences of abuse and neglect are as varied as the children who experience them. Not all consequences appear in all children. Some are mild, and some are severe. Some are short lived, and some are lifelong. They can be physical, psychological, or cognitive; each child could experience them in any combination. However, several factors affect individual outcomes of child maltreatment. Some of these are

- the child's age and developmental status at the time of the abuse or neglect,
- the type of maltreatment experienced (physical, sexual, neglect, etc.),
- the frequency, duration, and severity of the maltreatment, and
- the relationship between the child and the perpetrator (Child Information Gateway, 2013).

Another factor to consider is a child's resilience or lack thereof. Some children, despite similar situations, will experience lifelong consequences of their abuse, while others will be more able to cope and grow in a positive direction. This ability to move through these circumstances more positively is often referred to as *resilience*. This is not an innate characteristic, but one that comes from a mix of factors. Some factors thought to contribute to a maltreated child's resilience include positive attachment, self-esteem, intelligence, emotion regulation, independence, and humor (Shaffer, 2012). Because of this, it is difficult to predict the outcome of any one instance of abuse or neglect on a child. Outcomes for children with similar experiences of abuse could be very different. Each child brings to the situation his or her own genetic makeup; they bring their own temperament into the world. Once born, their heredity, or "nature" factor, as it can be called, comes into contact with their environment (the "nurture" factor). The intermingling of nature and nurture influences the consequences of maltreatment for a given child.

There is one final consequence to mention, and that is the cost of abuse and neglect on society as a whole. As stated by the Child Welfare Information Gateway (2013) "ultimately, due to related costs to public entities such as the health care, human services and educational systems, abuse and neglect impact not just the child and family, but society as a whole" (p. 7). Child maltreatment was found by the CDC to cost billions of dollars annually (www.childwelfare.gov, 2013). On top of that, there are long-term economic effects on society such as stress on the health care system, juvenile and adult criminal activity, domestic violence, employment, and financial problems resulting in need for public assistance, substance abuse, and mental illness. It must also be said that there are untold costs to society in terms of lost potential. What could these children have grown to achieve had they received a secure and loving childhood? No one will ever know for sure. Therefore, as individuals who work with children, we must strive to treat each child's case individually and not view them as a group—as "those poor maltreated children," who all behave similarly, and whose lives are surely ruined. If we do, opportunities to help these children grow and thrive may be missed. Those opportunities abound, and it is important to be on the lookout for them. Adults who achieve extreme success in the face of terrible conditions almost always point to some person or group whose support and guidance were crucial to their achievements. One never knows when one might be that person.

Chapter 2

The Role and Responsibilities of the Mandated Reporter

Julia A. Baxter

Regardless of the state in which you work, as a professional who is in a specifically suitable position to discern and suspect possible child maltreatment, you are required to report child abuse and neglect. Such persons are referred to as mandated reporters. According to the Child Welfare Information Gateway (2013), all states "have statutes identifying persons who are required to report suspected child maltreatment to an appropriate agency, such as child protective services, a law enforcement agency, or a state's toll-free child abuse reporting hotline" (p.1). Additionally, in most states, certain professions are designated as mandated by law to report child maltreatment due to the fact that individuals in those professions characteristically have regular contact with children. Among such mandated professionals are school personnel, including teachers, principals, counselors, and psychologists, to name a few. Other professions noted might be social workers, mental health professionals, child care providers, health care providers, law enforcement officials and coroners (Child Information Gateway, 2013). While the statues and their requirements vary by state, the concept of mandated reporting of child abuse and neglect is fairly standard throughout. At the end of this chapter, I have included information on mandated reporting for New York State as an example. To find out exactly what the laws are in other states, you can find links to that information in the Resources section of this text.

As far as school personnel are concerned, it would make perfect sense for them to be included on lists of mandated reporters for an assortment of reasons. Teachers often spend more time with children during week days than do parents and are in a position of knowing that child very well. As role models, teachers are often looked to for assistance, encouragement, and care. Most teachers have great concern for the health, happiness and well-being of their students and are aware that they have a responsibility to support this to the best of their ability. In their role as a mandated reporter, it is their duty to know how and when to make a report, what the various policies and procedures are, and that it is their charge to report suspected abuse and/or neglect (Crosson-Tower, 2003m). Not only is it the professionally ethical thing to do, in many states it is also the law.

The circumstances that cause a mandated reporter to make a hotline call may also vary from state to state. "Typically, a report must be made when the reporter, in his or her official capacity, suspects or has reason to believe that a child has been abused or neglected" or "institutions in which the reporter has knowledge of, or observes a child being subjected to, conditions that would reasonably result in harm to the child" (Child Information Gateway, 2013, p.3). Let us break that down for greater clarity:

1. **In your official capacity:** While acting within your position's role. For example, a school dance, a field trip, in your office or classroom.

2. **Suspects or has reason to believe:** Because you are trained to work with children, and due to the training, many states require for mandated reporters, you need only have a reasonable suspicion of maltreatment in order to report. This means that you do not need to have proof. You needn't have a list of evidence. There is not minimum requirement of items on a list to check off. The statues generally give the professional the ability to make the call when they feel that they have a reasonable cause to suspect the child is being maltreated.

3. **"Has knowledge of, or observes a child being subjected to conditions":** This refers to having been told something by a child or someone close to the child, or seeing something happen (perhaps a parent kicks, pushes or drags a child to the car by the arm roughly outside the school).

While statutes may vary in exact definitions of abuse and neglect, the procedures for calling, where to call, and when to report, the consensus is that a mandated reporter need only have a suspicion of abuse, and should make the report as soon as possible. "In any case, the intent is clear-incidents are to be reported as soon as they are noticed. Waiting for conclusive proof may involve further risk to the child" (Crosson-Tower, 2003, p.30).

HOW TO PREPARE FOR A REPORT

A good recommendation is to have some means of noting suspicions throughout your year. There may be something that seems odd to you. Perhaps something a student does or says is out of the ordinary for them. Perhaps they appear every Monday wearing the same dirty clothes they wore that past Friday. It may take weeks to have what you feel is a reasonable cause to suspect. Therefore, making note of your suspicion will help you when you finally do make the report. If something occurs that causes you to wonder, jot it down. Write down what it was and when it was. You may go back into your notes and see a pattern. If a student comes to school every other Monday with many "cat scratches" on their arms, and seems tired, distant and out of sorts on those days, write it down. By the second or third Monday, you may begin to wonder what is happening every other weekend. Sometimes, seeing it written down makes all the difference in being comfortable with your reason to suspect. Remember, though, that this is very confidential information. Wherever you note this information should remain secure at all times. Suspicions of child abuse are not to be lightly shared with other school staff in the faculty lounge, or outside of school. If you feel the need to consult another professional in your school, do so only to gain knowledge about that student (for example from a previous teacher), or to gain greater insight from a different professional such as the counselor if you are a teacher, or the teacher if you are the counselor. If you see something that you find troubling, it is a good idea to have the child visit the school nurse to have them look at it as well. The nurse not only has medical training but is also a mandated reporter. At times, having that extra collaboration is extremely useful in discerning the need to make a report.

Since procedures vary from state to state, it is vital to follow your state and school system's policies and guidelines for doing so. All states require an oral or written report, and some require both. This report goes to the agency responsible for their investigation and oversight of child abuse and neglect within the state. In most places, this agency is found within the state's department of social services, children and youth services, child protective services or some similar organization. In states where two reports are required, the oral report, or hotline call, is the most immediate; the written report is expected to follow that in a set period of time (for example 48 hours). The contents of the report may or may not be specified by the state, however if possible, the following information is good to have in front of you when making the report:

+ Name of the child
+ Age of the child
+ Gender of the child
+ Child's address
+ Who may be responsible for the abuse/neglect
+ Who lives in the home, including other minor children (sometimes it helps to know where they go to school and their grade levels)
+ What is the nature of the child's injuries, or what gave you cause to suspect
+ Any actions undertaken by the reporter, such as talking to the child, or consulting with past teachers, nurses, or counselors
+ Your name, contact information and where you work (your position). (Note: Sometimes, depending upon the state, you will not be required to give your name. In some states it is required.)

While all of the above information is quite helpful to the person evaluating the report, having less information should not prevent you from making the report. Child abuse reporting call centers are staffed by professionals who are trained to assist you through the process. If you forget something, they usually will ask questions to help you along. Overall, any information that you have about the child and his or her family that could potentially be valuable to the child protective service workers in their evaluation of the risk to the child is very beneficial.

WHEN DO I MAKE A REPORT?

Any education professional should make a report of child abuse or neglect as soon as they have a reasonable cause to suspect that maltreatment is occurring. I am frequently asked if this can be done too soon, or if one should wait until they are more certain something is happening. New educators, especially, are often very nervous about this process. They don't want to risk being wrong. Most advice I have encountered would suggest making the report as soon as the educator has a reasonable suspicion; the sooner the better. Remember, it is not your responsibility to KNOW if you are right. Your job here is to report your suspicion. The trained professionals whose job it is to screen these calls will make any further determinations. While it is not necessary to make a hotline call the moment you suspect maltreatment, if you feel that the child is in any imminent danger and may be at risk if they return home, try to make that call early in the day. This will allow the child protective services (CPS) worker to begin their investigation early in the day, making it more likely that an intervention could take place before school was over. Many state child abuse and neglect hotlines are staffed 24 hours a day, 7 days a week to enhance convenience for the reporter.

Just as every state has their own reporting procedures, they each have their own hotline numbers. Some states may have several, depending upon the size of their urban areas. Some states have specific hotlines dedicated only to taking calls from mandated reports, while others have one clearinghouse for all suspected child abuse reports, regardless of who is placing the call. It is a good idea to know the number which you are expected to call from your specific location, so that you are ready to report as soon as you see fit.

POSSIBLE ROADBLOCKS TO REPORTING

There are times when a reporter fails to make a hotline call due to internal concerns and beliefs or problems they face in their school environment. Despite what may be one's misgivings regarding making a report, it is vital that the teacher do so if abuse/ neglect is suspected. It is imperative to remember that a report of child abuse/neglect/ maltreatment is not an accusation of wrongdoing. It certainly feels that way. However, the hotline call is a request for professionals to discover if maltreatment has occurred and to start the process to assist in remedying that situation. Many factors come into play in the reporting process, and this may not always go as planned, nor be as easy as we would like. It is the combination of both internal and external feelings and difficulties that may result in making an educator reluctant to make a future report.

According to the U.S. Department of Health and Human Services manual for reporters of child maltreatment (2009), there are several major categories of such difficulties of which it is important to be aware.

1. **Personal feelings:** These include not wanting to get involved, worrying about the potential of angering parents, and fear of being in danger. These feelings are common and make sense. Additionally, the perpetrator of the abuse may

be someone known by the reporter. This makes it easy to talk oneself out of it. Remember, it is YOUR reasonable cause to suspect. Even if you know the family, and things "seem" fine on the outside, it doesn't mean that they are fine at all. It is good to make the report when there is a reasonable cause to suspect, in spite of any personal feelings to the contrary.

2. **Problems within the school**: There are some instances where the administration of a school may create obstacles to reporting child maltreatment. Some administrators may make it difficult to report, or even refuse to report suspected abuse. This can put the mandated reporter in a perilous position. Do they do what is legally required, or do they do what their administrator wants or tells them to do? This is a tough ethical situation to be in. In many States, this could also put the reporter in a position of possible legal ramifications. In New York, for example, the law states that the call is to be made by the person who suspects the maltreatment BEFORE notifying the building administrator. Furthermore, if the reporter does not make the call because they are dissuaded by the administration, in New York it remains their legal responsibility and they are liable if something happens to the child. As noted previously, familiarity with the procedures and statutes of the reporter's State and school district is vital. Be aware that you may have to discover this on your own, as many school districts fail to provide adequate training to their staff on reporting. I have found that since all educators in New York must be trained before certification, that further education is rarely provided. Therefore, it is often the reporter's responsibility to be aware of the requirements and possible barriers within the school. If a problem should arise, consultation with another school professional may assist you in working through this ethical dilemma, while not providing a disservice to your students in need of help

3. **Previous experiences reporting**: If a previous reporting experience went poorly or had a negative outcome, a reporter may be more reluctant to make a hotline call the next time. In some cases, the person on the other end of the call was rude, or unresponsive. In this instance, it is important to remember that the reporter can request to speak with an agency supervisor. Most states have protocol in place to give reporters that option if they are dissatisfied with the CPS professional with whom they are dealing. In addition, one negative experience does not mean that all subsequent experiences will also be negative. Regardless of having had negative past reporting experiences, the educator is still required to report any suspected child abuse or neglect. There are no exceptions to this. Please remember that while making a report in no way guarantees an improvement your student's situation, failure to report almost guarantees that the risk for this child will continue.

4. **Belief that nothing will be done**: Of all the excuses for not reporting child maltreatment, the one I hear the most out in the field is that "nothing will happen anyway, so why bother." While it is certainly frustrating to not have the outcome of a report be what was intended or desired, however, making the report creates a record of your suspicions and concerns. In addition, you will have discharged

your legal responsibility and transferred responsibility to child protection to discern what happens next. Some instances will require multiple reports before CPS feels they have enough cause to intervene. Again, it is not the reporter's job to discern the outcome of the call. It is the mandated reporter's responsibility to alert those who are charged with investigating claims of possible abuse or neglect.

WHAT HAPPENS AFTER A REPORT IS MADE?

The child maltreatment report sets off a sequence of events, which also varies by state, but tends to follow a similar process. The professionally trained person screening the call has several determinations to make. They must listen to the report and decide what to do next. If further follow-up is warranted, the child protective service worker in charge of the case must investigate the report. This often involves interviewing the child in question, as well as all of the minor children in that residence. After that, the adults are interviewed. Subsequently, the protective services professional must make a determination as to whether or not maltreatment is indicated. They assess the potential risk to the child or children. If the risk is minimal, they can implement interventions to assist the caregivers to better protect the child. If the risk is great, they impose more intrusive interventions, including removal of the child to a foster family for their protection if needed. A general sequence of events might look something like this (Crosson-Tower, 2003, p. 37):

1. Reporter has reasonable cause to suspect abuse or neglect.
2. Reporter follows state and school protocol and statutes for reporting and providing information to appropriate agency.
3. State worker performs intake to determine if report should be screened out or if it meets guidelines for investigation and considers urgency of the situation.
4. CPS assesses the situation, including speaking with the child and family, and assesses safety of the child and future risk of abuse and neglect.
5. Case is ruled indicated (or substantiated) or unfounded (or unsubstantiated).
6. If the case is indicated, CPS takes further measures that range from working with the family to address and remedy the situation to removing children from the home and arresting the perpetrator(s).
7. Services may continue for a period of time after which there is an evaluation of progress. If it is sufficient and the child is considered safe with no further intervention on the part of CPS, the case may be closed. If not, services may continue.
8. In the case of removal of children to foster care, more investigation and remediation is necessary prior to returning the children to the home. In some cases, it can involve changing the home situation (for example, having the heat and electricity turned back on, or cleaning up the home so that the child is again safe in the environment) as a requirement for return of the child. In extreme cases, the child may remain in foster care for a time period during which the caregivers may be found

to be unfit to have their children returned. In these cases, the adults' parental rights may be terminated, and the child may be freed for adoption. Many states require that every effort be made to reunite families wherever possible. However, this is not always possible (Crosson-Tower, 2003).

Mandated reporters often feel frustrated by the fact that they may receive little or no information about the case and its outcome after making a report. Due to state statutes surrounding privacy, state child protection agencies may not inform the reporter of the consequence of their call. Therefore, states vary widely regarding the amount of information that can be given back to the reporter. Some states require that child welfare agencies share findings with the reporter. This can be beneficial, because having the original reporter keep an eye on the situation to look for further evidence of child maltreatment can be very helpful to CPS. However, due to various laws surrounding confidentiality, it isn't always possible for CPS to inform the reporter of the status of the case, whether it is being investigated, or the result of any investigation. States vary in how much, if any, information can be shared with school personnel. This can be discouraging because as a caring educator, you want to know what is going on. Despite the potential lack of information, being supportive of the child at all times is often the only, and the best thing that can be done.

WHAT ARE THE LEGAL PROTECTIONS AND RAMIFICATION INVOLVED IN REPORTING?

A frequent concern is what might happen if one makes a report of maltreatment and it is found to be unsubstantiated by the child welfare agency. The good news here is that most states have laws that will protect the reporter from legal liability (such as being sued) as long as the report was made in good faith in accordance with the laws of their state. A problem would occur, then, if one were to make a report for malicious reasons. While this rarely happens, it is important to note that the reporter of any deliberately false report is not protected from any resulting liability. Additionally, there might be ramifications on the school level.

Most states have, as part of their statutes, penalties on mandated reporters for failure to report child abuse and neglect according to their mandated reporter laws. This can range from a criminal charge (a misdemeanor in New York and many other states) and associated penalties (such as jail time and monetary fines), to no protection for the reporter should a civil court case arise (ncsl.org, n.d.). There is an important distinction to note here. These penalties apply to reporters who willfully do not make a report of suspected abuse or neglect. This involves the knowing intent of the reporter to do nothing in a situation that calls for action. This differs greatly from not being aware. There are many instances where the educator has no idea abuse or neglect is occurring. Many families do an excellent job of hiding any maltreatment. Children come to school clean, are well behaved, and seem fine in class. Parents or caregivers may seem attentive and supportive. However, what goes on behind closed doors may be a very different story. In one case I knew of, the abusive parents were both teaching in the school the child attended. No one suspected anything until a family member spoke out. In cases such as this, it is common to feel like you let the child down; like you failed in your duty to protect your student. Be aware that it would not be possible for even the best trained educator to notice every possible case of abuse or neglect. All you can do is to make the best determination possible with your level of training and the information evident to you.

WHAT HAPPENS IF A CHILD IS PUT INTO FOSTER CARE?

The Child Welfare Information Gateway (April, 2015) noted that there were over 400,000 children in foster care at the time of their 2013 study. The Code of Federal Regulations (2012) defines foster care as "24-hour substitute care for children outside their own homes" (Title 45, Volume 4, Part 1355, Section 57). According to kidsdata.org (n.d.)

> Foster care is intended to provide temporary, safe living arrangements and therapeutic services for children who cannot remain safely at home due to child maltreatment or for children whose parents are unable to provide adequate care. The U.S. foster care system aims to safely reunify children with their parents or secure another permanent home, e.g., through adoption. However, too often this goal is not achieved. Instead, many children spend years in foster homes or group homes, often moving multiple times. These children are at increased risk for a variety of emotional, physical, behavioral, and academic problems (Why This Topic is Important, para. 1).

When the environment and/or circumstances in which the child is living are a serious threat to the child, the child may need to be removed from their home and placed into this new setting. This is one possible result of an investigation when a report of child abuse is made. In New York State, the child is placed into a foster home in the county where the child resides. This home may not be in the school district that the child was attending, causing the child to enter a new school setting. This means that the student you reported may no longer be in your classroom. You may also have a new student in your classroom because of their move into foster care.

If your report of child abuse leads to the placement of your student in foster care in another school district, you may experience a sense of grief and loss. You may feel guilty for being the catalyst that led to the child's removal from a familiar school setting. These are normal reactions. If you are struggling with your own emotions or with explaining the situation to students who are missing their friend, the school counselor is an excellent resource for you. It is good to talk this over with the counselor if you feel the need. Additionally, you can ask the school counselor to explain the student's absence from your class if you find it difficult to do so yourself. Professionals in a school environment are meant to work as collaborative teams. In situations like this, it is valuable to access those in your school who have the expertise to help you and your students to deal with this.

When receiving a new student into your school as a result of a foster care placement, the school counselor or social worker will be a vital source of support for the student as they are working through this major transition. These children need to feel welcomed and safe, and it is important to do whatever you can to ensure their comfort in their new scholastic setting. Many of the suggestions in the section on supporting abused children will be helpful if you are dealing with this scenario.

WHAT DO I DO IF A CHILD DISCLOSES TO ME?

The previous lists of possible indicators of child abuse and neglect are ponderous to say the least. However, each list ends with "the child reports being" … abused, neglected, etcetera. If a child does disclose maltreatment to you, what do you? How should you handle it? It can be scary to have a child tell you that they are being maltreated. Millions of thoughts run through your mind: "Are they telling the truth?"; "What do I do now?"; "How should I react?" This anxiety can be magnified by knowing that the reaction of the first person to whom a child discloses has a tremendous impact on how the child will do in the future. Therefore, handling this scenario as well as possible is crucial to the child's overall well-being. Think for a moment, if you will, of a time when you shared something very personal with someone or asked for something you were frightened to ask for. Did you tell a parent that you cheated on a test or that you skipped school? Did you ask someone you really liked out on a date or to the prom? Did you share a personal memory or health issue with a partner? How did you feel before you did this? Were you scared? Worried? Afraid of what the person you told would think of you? Fearful of rejection? Conjure up those feelings and magnify them and you can put yourself in the shoes of a child who has decided to disclose this horrible secret to an adult. It's terrifying for some children. Perhaps they were threatened by the perpetrator or worried that you won't believe them or like them anymore. They might be afraid you will blame them or that you won't care. I, for one, didn't discuss my childhood abuse with anyone outside of my family until I was 31. I thought that this was something I had to endure to maintain some semblance of a brave façade; I wanted to be someone else. I felt that if people knew what was inside of me they wouldn't want to know me. I felt that I would be even more unlovable than I already felt that I was. If a child or adolescent chooses you to disclose to, it is not only a huge honor, but also an immense responsibility. Following a few simple guidelines will help the professional navigate this important interaction.

First and foremost, if a child begins by saying something like "I need to tell you something, but you have to PROMISE not to tell anyone. Do you promise?" Even though you want to say, "Of course I do!" as you look into the child's scared and pleading eyes, you simply cannot. As mandated reporters of child abuse and neglect, you are bound by law to report a disclosure according to the state regulations by which you are governed. If you say you WILL keep their secret no matter what and then they disclose abuse to you, you cannot keep that secret. You must then either tell them that you cannot keep that secret (and that you have actually lied to them by saying you would), or you don't tell them and report it anyway, which they will most likely figure out, again, leading to feeling lied to. Both of these scenarios can be damaging. Therefore, it is better to be honest up front by saying something like "Of course I will keep your secret. … unless you or someone else is being hurt or is in danger. Then I have to tell someone because part of my job is keeping you safe." Many have asked me if this can lead the child to decide not to disclose. The answer is yes it can. However, lying to the child in order to get them to disclose is potentially quite emotionally damaging. As a school counselor, I was told to begin sessions by telling each child about confidentiality and having to tell if someone was being hurt or in danger. It is, ethically, the right thing to do.

One excellent model to follow in a situation where a child reveals to you that they are being abused is the BASER model (Henderson, 1992 as cited in Florida Institute of Technology Family Learning Program Information About Sexual Abuse, n.d., research. fit.edu.). The basis of the model is to remember that it is your job to reassure the child that they did the right thing by telling you and that you don't judge them. You need to let them know that there is help available and that you are going to talk to people who can help them (FIT Family Learning Program, research.fit.edu). The points below explain how to follow the BASER (Henderson, 1992, p. 8):

1. **BELIEVE the child:**
   + The child needs to feel that you believe them even if you don't. You can actually tell the child that you believe what they are saying, "I believe what you are telling me." If you have doubts, simply tell them that you are listening. Don't judge. Don't question. Don't interrogate. Remain open and empathetic. This child could be known for telling tall tales, but it is not up to you to discern the truth or validity of this disclosure. Your job is to listen and report. Investigating the validity of the disclosure is up to those whose job it is to follow up on child abuse reports.

2. **AFFIRM the disclosure:**
   + Telling someone is scary. You need to let them know that they did the right thing by telling you: "I'm glad that you told me." "Thank you for telling me. That must have been really hard."

3. **SUPPORT the child:**
   + Give the child support in a variety of forms. Let them know that this is in no way their fault. Children often feel that they did something to deserve the abuse or maltreatment. Often, they are told so. Tell the child that you are there for them.

4. **EMPOWER the child:**
   + "There are some things we can do to help you feel better again." Tell them about what is going to happen next and that there are other people who will help them.

5. **REPORT the case:**
  + The child needs to know that you are going to report this. Tell them in a developmentally appropriate manner that it is part of your job to do this, and that it is part of getting them the help they need to be safe. I have had many instances of children getting upset when they realize that this is what is going to happen. However, you can't tell them that you won't report it even if they ask you to. You are not asking their permission to report. This can be tough, but you need to stay calm and focused and remind them that they deserve to be safe and that you want to help them. By reporting, you are involving people whose jobs are to keep children safe.

Besides the BASER model (Henderson, 1992 as cited in FIT Family Learning Program Information About Sexual Abuse, n.d.), there are additional guidelines when talking to children about abuse. The Rape, Abuse and Incest National Network (RAINN) suggests that you strive to create a non-threatening environment in which the child will feel more comfortable and able to open up. According to RAINN (rainn.org) the following guidelines will help you to create this atmosphere during your conversation:

  + **Pick your time and place carefully:** This is something that needs to be done in a comfortable space, and not in front of other people (especially those who may be harming the child).
  + **Be aware of your tone of voice:** If your tone is too serious, you might scare the child further. Keep it more casual and very non-threatening. Try to keep judgment, sarcasm, fear, and an overly serious tone at bay. Don't react with disgust, shock, or anger. Empathy and support is the key here if you want to encourage the child to talk to you.
  + **Talk directly to the child:** You can't ask leading questions, nor interrogate. You can't say, "Is someone touching you?" It could be considered a leading question. However, if the child tells you that someone is touching them, a good follow up would be, "What do you mean by touching?" Use language that is clear and understandable to the child.
  + **Listen carefully and follow up:** Allow the child to talk openly and freely. Don't worry about word choice or grammar. Listen intently. Wait for them to pause before you talk, and then follow up on the pieces of what they are saying that have you feeling concerned. "I hear you saying that your father is hurting you. I'm sorry to hear that. Can you tell me more about that?" Remember that the word *hurt* could mean totally different things to the child and to you. Follow up and let them tell you what they mean.
  + **Avoid all judgment and blame:** Use *I* questions and statements to help you avoid placing any judgment. "I'm concerned by what you said" is less potentially judgmental than "You said something that really upset me" Refrain from asking *why* questions, as this forces them to think of reasons for the abuse and may lead to them feeling at fault.

- **Reassure the child**: Make sure the child knows that it was the right thing to have told you. Confirm their feelings. Let them know it is OK to feel scared, upset, hurt, confused, or angry.
- **Be patient**: This may not be a quick and easy conversation. Be patient and kind as the child speaks. The child may be terrified of what will happen to them if they tell, especially if the perpetrator has threatened them. I had a child once tell me that he had been warned about people like me. He had been told if he shared his stories with "people like me" that he and his sister would be taken away, he would be separated from his sister, and he would never see her again. He wasn't willing to chance that, and he never did choose to disclose anything to me of the horrors that we eventually discovered were happening to him.

Regardless of what you feel is happening, it is ultimately the child's decision to disclose to you or not. You cannot MAKE them disclose to you. You can open the door to the conversation. You can ask if they are OK. You can tell them that you care and that you are there for them if they ever want to talk. If and when they do decide to talk to you, you will be ready. An excellent piece of guidance comes from the Florida Institute of Technology's Family Learning Program (FLP), (n.d., research.fit.edu). Do your best not to show that you are upset by their story because the child may take that to mean that you are upset with them or that this is worse than they thought it was. Don't make judgments. These may create more anxiety and fear and might actually be opposite to what the child thinks or wants. Be caring, but do not assume that you know exactly how the child is feeling. Let them talk. Listen to them and ask them to share what they are thinking and feeling. The child, above all, needs to feel heard and supported.

HOW DO I HELP AND SUPPORT CHILDREN WHO HAVE BEEN ABUSED OR MALTREATED?

There are many myths and platitudes spoken about children who have been maltreated, neglected, or traumatized. "They will never remember it; they are too young." "They'll grow out of it." "Kids are resilient; they bounce back." "The abuse has stopped now, so they should be fine." "She never talks about it, so I guess it doesn't bother her." "It's best to never talk about it; that way he can forget about it." These are just a few things to be overheard regarding the children of abuse. Children can be very resilient, but they are not unbreakable. Artifacts of the experiences remain long after the episodes of maltreatment have ceased. These children continue to have lives. They go to school, play on sports teams, act in plays, and take dance classes. As a mandated reporter of child abuse and neglect, it can be very frustrating to be aware that making that hotline call is the only thing the law asks you to do. You are required to report suspected child maltreatment. Many times, the report leads nowhere and nothing in the child's life changes. This can be disheartening and lead to feelings of hopelessness. While it is true that the system is not perfect, it is a far cry from where we were in the 1960's. After the report is made and regardless of the outcome, there are many things that you can do to help children who have experienced neglect, pain, abuse, trauma, and hardships.

All professionals who work with children can support positive growth in abused children. However, school professionals and teachers, are particularly able to help children to work through their difficult situations, and to help them to become more resilient. The cornerstone of this ability is the creation of a positive school climate and classroom environment. Schools can and should provide a safe haven for children whose home lives are fraught with fear, pain, loneliness, criticism, and hunger. Educators are already overburdened with content, assessment, lessons, management, and more. The thought of having to also help abused children can be overwhelming and distressing. As fittingly noted by Bancroft (1997), "It's not that I believe that teachers … can solve the problem, or that reporting suspected child abuse always leads to an improved situation for the child, or that it's possible to intervene in every case. But teachers make a huge difference. Teachers can provide an effective counterbalance to the effects of an abusive home. It does not require special heroism" (p. 69). Superhero capacity aside, there are many things that an educator can do to help abused and neglected children to be more successful in the classroom, feel more hopeful about their futures, be more resilient, make better decisions, and have better self-esteem.

In addition to having a very safe and positive classroom environment, there are many things that can be done to help maltreated children in a school and classroom setting. First of all, it is imperative to be mindful that children who have experienced threat and trauma may be challenging to have in one's classroom. As discussed previously, educators should know that living in a fear state can foster many neurological and emotional behaviors and cognitive consequences. Perry (n.d.) summed it up well.

> When we are under threat, our minds and bodies will respond in an adaptive fashion, making changes in our state of arousal (mental state), our style of thinking (cognition) and in our body's physiology (e.g., increased heart rate, muscle tone, rate of respiration). To understand how we respond to threat it is important to appreciate that as we move along the arousal continuum— from calm to arousal to alarm, fear and terror—different areas of our brain control and orchestrate our mental and physical functioning. The more threatened we become, the more 'primitive' (or regressed) our style of thinking and behaving becomes. When a traumatized child is in a state of alarm (because they are thinking about the trauma, for example) they will be less capable of concentrating, they will be more anxious, and they will pay more attention to 'non-verbal' cues such as tone of voice, body posture and facial expressions. This has important implications for understanding the way the child is processing, learning, and reacting in a given situation. (Perry, n.d., para. 1)

With this in mind, what are some of the best ways to provide support for abused and neglected children? The following guidelines, as offered by Bear, Schenk and Buckner (1992) should provide some assistance in this endeavor (pp. 46–47).

1. **Expectations:** Continue to have high expectations. But remember, heightened emotions and hypervigilance can interfere with thinking. Therefore, it is good to set reasonable goals for abused children, and then to provide sufficient support to enable them to achieve these goals. Doing this will help children feel more confident of their abilities, and to consequently be able to see themselves as more successful. Make sure that your expectations for behavior are very clear, and the child understands both the rules and the consequences for breaking them. Be consistent with consequences and demonstrate both flexibility and understanding where appropriate. Use positive reinforcement and rewards over punishment wherever possible (Perry, n.d.).

2. **Structure:** The pattern for the day should be both predictable and consistent. As stated by Bear, Schenk and Buckner (1992): "Abused children may feel powerless to control much in their environment. To cope, they may: (a) refuse to even try to control what happens around them; (b) strive to manipulate everything they can by bossing peers and controlling belongings; and (c) express disproportionate feelings whenever they feel threatened" (p. 46.). Then these children overreact to a situation seemingly out of nowhere, possibly as an attempt to regain or establish control. When this occurs, it is important to give children a sense of control in a positive way. It is therefore important to give them accurate information, such as the pattern for the day or if there will be any changes in activities or staff. If the child becomes anxious, allow them to appropriately express their feelings whenever possible. Good mediums for this include drama, creative writing, and art. Another way of helping a child with the concept of control is to give them a choice, if possible, in an activity or interaction. Even if the choice isn't pleasant, having some control can be helpful. An example would be, "You have a choice: you can finish your math seatwork now, or you can finish it when the class is having free time." Sometimes, just reframing the interaction can help the child feel more in control and less anxious (Perry, n.d.).

3. **Identity:** Children who have been maltreated may struggle with personal identity. Teachers can help here by capitalizing on a student's strengths and helping them to use those in areas in which they are weaker. Some statements that can help with this include, "You are a really hard worker"; "I saw how you helped him"; or "You are a really good friend"; "One reason we like having you in class is that you are so fun to be with". Such comments can help the child understand that others see them positively. Another way to help the child establish personal identity is to ask them about their interests and opinions, and to teach them problem-solving and decision-making skills. The goal is for children to have a better sense of self-understanding.

4. **Self-esteem:** This is probably one of the biggest areas a teacher can help with. Abused children quite frequently have very low self-esteem; they do not value themselves, nor see value in themselves. Teachers are in an excellent position to help children feel that they are valued and capable and accepted. This can be

accomplished by setting up an environment in which uniqueness is honored and differences are valued. This enables children to see themselves as someone who has something to offer. Successful completion of tasks in a classroom can help the child to feel competent. Feeling competent, accepted, valued, and contributing to the classroom will all work toward increasing the child's self-esteem.

5.   **Sense of belonging:** Many abused children feel like they are bad people who don't belong. They require a very nurturing, comforting, and inclusive environment. Teachers should, therefore, strive to foster a sense of belonging. Displaying children's artwork prominently in the classroom and working to ensure that all students are included in classroom activities are two possible ways of accomplishing this. It is also helpful if children have their own personal spaces for their possessions, such as a desk, locker, or cubby.

6.   **Social skills:** Social skills may be lacking in children of abuse and neglect. If they have not learned to listen to their inner selves, they may only focus on meeting the needs of and pleasing others. In addition, the abusive background may have taught the child inappropriate language, behaviors, or ways of dealing with conflicts. Teaching social skills directly and modeling appropriate ways of interacting may be quite helpful here.

7.   **Tolerance of differences:** Every child responds in her or his own way to the abuse or maltreatment they received. Therefore, behaviors in the classroom may vary greatly. The child may be experiencing anxiety, guilt, embarrassment, or anger. A classroom environment that promotes an appreciation of differences can be very helpful in making all children feel accepted. Remember that if you see some behaviors that you think might be related to abuse, it is a good idea to consult with another professional at your school, such as the psychologist, nurse, or counselor.

8.   **Consistency:** Like structure, consistency is fostered by having clear expectations for behavior and performance, as well as a daily schedule that provides clear structure. With consistency and structure, a child is more likely to take risks and overcome some of the fear that is often an abused child's constant companion.

Teachers have the opportunity to give an abused child the hope of a childhood, the joy of play, and the sense of being cared for by others. Those are gifts that cannot be measured in any monetary or quantitative way. (Bear, 1992, p.47)

SCENARIOS AND PERSONAL ACCOUNTS

Among the best ways to prepare for being a mandated reporter of child abuse and neglect is the use of scenarios, examples, and personal accounts. There are many resources for this available online, as well as several excellent first-person narratives regarding abuse (one example is Stolen Innocence, by Erin Merryn, 2005). I would encourage anyone interested in adding to the depth of their understanding of child abuse and reporting to seek out such resources.

In my research, I found that many good scenarios are available as part of mandated child abuse training modules online for certain states. Two that I thought were particularly useful were from Virginia and Georgia. They can be found at:

http://www.dss.virginia.gov/family/cps/mandated_reporters/cwse5691/story_html5.html

http://www.cobbk12.org/childabusereport/

NEW YORK MANDATED CHILD ABUSE REPORTING

New York, as is the case with all states, has a law requiring mandated reporting of child abuse and neglect by professionals whose positions put them in contact with children and who have training which makes them particularly equipped to do so. According to this state's law, many professionals in New York are required to report child abuse, including those who work in hospitals, schools, day care centers, and law enforcement (The entire current list can be found in Article 6, Title 6, Section 413 of the New York Social Services Law, which can be accessed online through the New York State Legislature's Website [public.leginfo.state.ny.us/menuf.cgi and click on Laws of New York to access Social Services Law.]). In New York, many professionals must complete mandated child abuse training in order to qualify for licensure or certification in their profession (such as licensed social workers and mental health care professionals, certified teachers, school counselors, school nurses and school psychologists (Pub. 1159 [Rev. 5/2015]).

What follows is a summary of what mandated child abuse reporters need to know about the law governing them in New York State (New York State Office of Child and Family Services [NYSOCSF], http://ocfs.ny.gov).

When are you Mandated to Report?
According to the law, mandated reporters are

> required to report suspected child abuse or maltreatment when they are presented with **reasonable cause to suspect** (*emphasis mine*) child abuse or maltreatment in a situation where a child, parent, or other person legally responsible for the child is before the mandated reporter when the mandated reporter is acting in his or her official or professional capacity (NYSOCFS, 2015).

As is the case with many laws, this requires some further explanation to make it clear.

+ *Reasonable cause to suspect:* According to the New York State Office of Child and Family Services (2015)

> Reasonable cause to suspect child abuse or maltreatment means that, based on your rational observations, professional training, and experience, you have a suspicion that the parent or other person legally responsible for a child is responsible for harming that child or placing that child in imminent

danger of harm. Your suspicion can be as simple as distrusting an explanation for an injury (p. 2).

This means that you, as a professional who has training and education, should make a report if you feel that you have a reasonable cause to believe that the child is being abused or maltreated. This phrase leaves the door open for you to use your professional judgment to decide to make a report. You do not need proof. You do not need a statement from someone. You just need to have a reasonable suspicion that abuse, or neglect is happening. This is worded thusly to encourage professionals to make a report even if they don't feel positive that something is happening. Don't worry if you make a report, and it is not investigated. That is up to the state to decide. If you feel the need to report something, you should do so.

+ ***Other person legally responsible:*** This refers to a guardian, caretaker, or other person 18 years of age or older who is responsible for the care of the child. It is important to note that this person need not be the parent. If another adult over 18 has custodial care of the child at the time of the abuse or neglect, it doesn't matter if that person is the parent or legal guardian. This could be, for example, a babysitter, or a parent's partner, or live in friend or companion who has custodial care of the child at the time of the incident.

+ ***Professional capacity:*** This means that you are working in your professional role while presented with this reasonable cause to suspect child abuse or neglect. For example, a teacher who sees a child with suspicious bruises every Monday for which there are no adequate explanations and, therefore, has a reasonable suspicion of abuse must report the concern. A teacher out in a local park on the weekend while "off duty" is not mandated to report abuse of a child they saw with bruises. "The mandated reporter's legal responsibility to report suspected child abuse or maltreatment ceases when the mandated reporter stops practicing his/her profession" (NYSOCSF, 2015, p. 2). In cases where you see something outside of your professional capacity, you may still report the abuse to the non-mandated reporter hotline. New York State encourages everyone to report suspicions of child abuse or neglect at any time.

What do you Report?

The indicators of possible abuse and neglect are well covered in the previous pages of this chapter. However, New York does have specific definitions of abuse and neglect. As stated by the NYSOCFS (2015, p. 2):

Abuse
An abused child is one whose parent or other person legally responsible for his or her care inflicts serious physical injury upon the child, creates a substantial risk of serious physical injury, or commits a sex offense against the child. Abuse also includes situations

where a parent or other person legally responsible knowingly allows someone else to inflict such harm on a child.

Maltreatment (Includes Neglect)
Maltreatment means that a child's physical, mental, or emotional condition has been impaired, or placed in imminent danger of impairment, by the failure of the child's parent or other person legally responsible to exercise a minimum degree of care by failing to provide

- sufficient food, clothing, shelter, or education;
- proper supervision, guardianship, or medical care (refers to all medical issues, including dental, optometric, and surgical care); or
- inflicting excessive corporal punishment, abandoning the child, or misusing alcohol or other drugs to the extent that the child was placed in imminent danger.

Note: Poverty or other financial inability to provide the above is not maltreatment.

Emotional Maltreatment
The summary of the legal definition in New York State (Prevent Child Abuse New York, 2009):

> Impairment of emotional health and impairment of mental or emotional condition includes a state of substantially diminished psychological or intellectual functioning in relation to, but not limited to, such factors as failure to thrive, control of aggressive or self-destructive impulses, ability to think and reason, or acting out and misbehavior …; provided, however, that such impairment must be clearly attributable to the unwillingness or inability of the parent or other person legally responsible for the child to exercise a minimum degree of care toward the child. (p.4)

This makes proving emotional maltreatment very difficult in New York. That being said, one should always report it if there is reasonable cause to suspect.

Sexual Abuse
The summary of the legal definition in New York State (Prevent Child Abuse New York, 2009) is

> A sexually abused child is a child less than eighteen years of age whose parent— or other person legally responsible for his/her care—commits or allows to be committed a sex offense against such child, or as defined by the Penal law; commits incest, allows, permits, or encourages such child to engage in acts or conduct which constitute prostitution or a sexual performance. (p. 3)

When and Where Do I Call to Make a Report?

In New York State, a mandated reporter of child abuse and neglect is urged to make the call as soon as they feel that there is a reasonable cause to suspect that it is occurring in a child's life. It is important to remember that your call is what starts the process that may lead to an intervention by a local child protective service unit. Therefore, the sooner you make the call, the sooner CPS staff from a local social services department can begin looking into it.

According to the New York State Office of Child and Family Services, (retrieved March 10, 2017 from http://ocfs.ny.gov/main/cps/faqs.asp#reportl), the calls are placed mainly to the State Central Register of Child Abuse and Maltreatment, or the SCR as it is often called. The SCR is staffed by child protective specialists who are available to take calls at any time of the day, seven days a week. Depending on where in New York State you work, you may have the option to call a hotline that is run by the county (such as in Onondaga County), so it is best to find out that specific number when you are hired at a school in New York.

The telephone numbers to report abuse or maltreatment in New York (as of this printing) are:

+ Mandated Reporter Hotline: (800) 635-1522
+ Public Hotline: (800) 342-3720

Another important factor regarding the placement of hotline calls is that you are not required to notify parents or other custodial care givers that you are going to place a call or that you have placed a call. In fact, it is not recommended that you notify the persons legally responsible for the child at all regarding your report. Alerting a parent or other person legally responsible for the child of the report can actually create problems for the investigation that could negatively affect the ability of local CPS workers to discern the child's safety. In a worst-case scenario, it could even put the child's safety at risk.

What Happens When I Call the SCR?

Making a report of child abuse or maltreatment can certainly cause some anxiety in the reporter. My experience has been that the trained CPS specialist who takes your call is well aware of this and is ready to help walk you through the process. They will ask you to give them as much information as you have, such as the name and county where the child resides, the nature and extent of the injuries or the risk of harm to the child, and information regarding any other minor children living in the residence that you know of. While it is always better to have as much information as possible, you are encouraged to make a hotline call even if you have little information. The professionals who take these calls will work with the information you give them to determine if it is adequate to require them to register a report.

When you make the call, I always suggest keeping a record of this for yourself. I always write down the date and time of my call, to whom I spoke (you can ask for their name), and the call's ID number. Ask the SCR specialist for that number and keep it in your records.

After you make your report, the SCR staff may discern that the information does not, at this time, warrant the need to register the child abuse or maltreatment report. This reason should be explained to you clearly. If you do not feel that this was handled properly, or disagree greatly with the decision, you may ask to speak to the CPS specialist's supervisor. Supervisors are trained to assist in making determinations and can be of help in difficult cases.

If the SCR registers your call, the department of social services in the child's county of residence is then notified. Be aware that this is NOT the county in which the school is located, but the county in which the child resides. This is especially important for school districts that enroll for more than one county. Within 24 hours of your initial call, a CPS caseworker will begin an investigation by visiting the child's school and interviewing not only the child, but all of the minor children who live in that household and attend the school. CPS caseworkers do not need parental permission to interview a child in their school. The caseworker will evaluate the child and other children and create a plan to best meet the needs of the child. However, if there is an immediate threat to a child's safety, health, or life, CPS may elect to remove the child from their home (or in severe cases, not allow them to return home from the school setting).

If you make a hotline call that results in the removal of the child from their home, be aware that this may involve the placement of a child in a foster home that is not in your school district. This can be very upsetting for both you and the students in the child's class. If this happens, you may want to consult with a school counselor or social worker as to the best way to address this in your classroom. You may feel guilty that your report has resulted in the child's removal from their home and school. However, remember that these determinations are made by highly trained professionals and are not made lightly. If you find yourself very upset or overwhelmed by this, it would be good to seek the counsel of a professional in your school who could help you with these feelings.

Law Enforcement Referrals

Not all scenarios are considered appropriate for investigation by child protective services. If the hotline call contains information that includes a crime committed against or a threat to a child and the perpetrator is not the custodial care giver (parent or other person legally responsible for the child), then the SCR makes a law enforcement referral. In this case, your information is recorded and sent on to the New York State Police who will handle any further investigation.

The Protection of People with Special Needs Act

The Protection of People with Special Needs Act requires persons who are mandated reporters under that act to report abuse, neglect, and significant incidents involving vulnerable persons to the Vulnerable Persons' Central Register (VPCR) operated by the New York State Justice Center for the Protection of People with Special Needs (http://www.justicecenter.ny.gov/).

Under the act, persons who are mandated reporters to the Statewide Central Register of Child Abuse and Maltreatment are also mandated reporters to the VPCR, with the exception of day care providers and staff. Day care providers and staff are mandated reporters to the SCR, but not to the VPCR.

Effective June 30, 2013, persons who are mandated reporters under the act have a legal duty to

- report to the Justice Center, by calling the VPCR at 1+(855) 373-2122, if they have reasonable cause to suspect abuse or neglect of a vulnerable person, including any person receiving residential services in a facility operated by, or provider agency facility licensed or certified by, the Office of Children and Family Services (OCFS);
- report all significant incidents regarding vulnerable persons to the Justice Center by calling the VPCR at 1+(855) 373-2122; and
- continue to call the Statewide Central Register of Child Abuse and Maltreatment if they have reasonable cause to suspect abuse or maltreatment of children in family and foster homes, and day care settings. Suspicion of child abuse or maltreatment in a day care setting, foster care, or within a family home must continue to be reported to the Statewide Center Register of Child Abuse and Maltreatment at 1+(800) 635-1522.

Protections and Liabilities

As stated in the Summary Guide for Mandated Reporters of New York State (2016) the following protections and liabilities apply to mandated reporters of child abuse and neglect in New York State:

Immunity for Liability

"If a mandated reporter makes a report with earnest concern for the welfare of a child, he or she is immune from any criminal or civil liability that might result" (p. 4). This is what is known as a report in good faith.

Protection from Retaliatory Personnel Action

Section 413 of the Social Services Law states that "no medical or other public or private institution, school, facility or agency shall take any retaliatory personnel action against an employee who made a report to the SCR. Furthermore, no school, school official, child care provider, foster care provider, or mental health facility provider shall impose any conditions, including prior approval or prior notification, upon a member of their staff mandated to report suspected child abuse or maltreatment" (p. 4).

Penalties for Failure to Report

A mandated reporter of child abuse and neglect, as defined in New York State Law, who fails to make such a report "could be charged with a Class A misdemeanor and subject to criminal penalties. Further, mandated reporters can be sued in civil court for monetary damages for any harm caused by the mandated reporter's failure to make the report to the SCR" (p. 4)

All mandated reporters who require licensure or certificated through the New York State Department of Education (NYSED) are required to take mandated reporter training as a condition of that licensure or certification.

For Additional Information:
New York State Office of Child and Family Services: http://ocfs.ny.gov
http://ocfs.ny.gov/main/publications/pub1159.pdf
www.nysmandatedreporter.org
http://ocfs.ny.gov/main/JusticeCenter/default.asp

MANDATED CHILD ABUSE REPORTING IN OTHER STATES

As previously indicated, the majority of states have some manner of mandated child abuse reporting law. Most educators are seen as professionals whose jobs put them in a position to suspect possible abuse and neglect; most are required to report as part of their positions. This chapter looked not only at child abuse and neglect information for all education professionals, but it also included information on mandatory reporting of child abuse and neglect for educators in New York State. Mandatory reporting training is required to receive a state education certification.

If you are interested in the various laws and policies pertaining to child abuse and neglect reporting in other states, the best resource I have found is from the Child Welfare Information Gateway. Their report on state statutes (current through 2013) can be found here: https://www.childwelfare.gov/systemwide/laws_policies/state/

If you seek further information about the mandated reporting laws pertaining to education in each state, please visit that state's Department of Education's website. It should have links to mandated reporting information for that state.

Chapter 3

Child-Specific Expressions of Stress Disorder Signs

William E. Krill

The dual challenge is to first understand the signs and symptoms that are specific to children with PTSD, and then those signs and symptoms specific to one particular child. As mentioned earlier, in my clinical experience, children, especially young children, seem to have behavioral expressions of stress disorder that look different than those of adults with stress disorder. At first glance, the broad strokes of symptom identification [...] look pretty much the same. But when individual expressions or discrete behaviors are observed, children will have behaviors that adults generally do not have, or rarely have. The six areas of behavioral stress disorder signs need to be viewed through the developmental level of the child.

It is almost axiomatic that children will have some quantity or quality differences in behavioral expressions than adults do, even when both share the same mental health disorder. A stark example of the behavioral differences between adults and children is the fact that the majority of stress disorder cases that I have dealt with in very young children have all had wetting/soiling issues (beyond the potty learning age) that have not responded to the usual forms of therapeutic intervention. In many of these cases, the child not only is *encopretic* (having involuntary defecation not attributable to physical defects or illness), but also engages in feces manipulation or smearing.

Children's behavioral expressions of stress disorder are complicated by the fact that they are children: many adults will chalk up the behaviors that they see as other, more common childhood behaviors such as stubbornness, being spoiled, or "tantrums". Each of these behaviors, when viewed through the lens of PTSD and the perspective of developmental limitations, transform into something a bit more complicated. Indeed, one of the telling signs that a child may be suffering from PTSD is that the ordinary applications of guidance and discipline (not to mention medication) do not seem to be effective.

In addition, the child's relative level of development in all spheres must also be taken into consideration; what may appear to be a severely immature child may be a child who once had near age-appropriate maturity, but now is experiencing regressions due to trauma. The child's basic developmental level appears to have impact on the behavioral signs, especially those signs that have to do with ego cohesion. The younger the child, the less primary, healthy ego development they have gained prior to the trauma.

PHYSIOLOGICAL SIGNS

Often, children demonstrate very rapid onset of physical and emotional agitation with equally rapid change back to relative calmness. Caretakers and clinicians will describe this effect as a "light switch". One moment, the child will be calm and happy, the next moment extremely upset and inconsolable, or agitated and aggressive.

This is followed by a rather rapid calming and the child switching back to a happy child. Also, the child may appear to have little memory about the upset or what caused it. Another pattern seems to be that the child becomes physically and emotionally agitated, with waves of upset, and may stay that way for extended periods of time (hours or days.)

This may be followed once again by a relatively calm period of days or weeks. It is easy to see how one might think that the child may have Attention-Deficit Hyperactivity Disorder (ADHD) or bi-polar disorder. Misdiagnosis may be due to the psychologist not receiving the information needed concerning a specific trauma event to make them aware of a stress disorder possibility. The parent of the child may conveniently forget the important event, or, the family may have a long history of multiple, smaller stressors that are simply taken as non-sequitur in their lives.

A fairly typical stress episode seen in young children with PTSD follows a pattern such as this: either an internal or external cue triggers the biological reaction, the child begins to escalate in emotional and physical agitation, the stress peaks, and then the child reaches a point of exhaustion that may proceed either to tears, sleep, or a very rapid "light switch" return to normalcy. The whole process may be only a matter of moments, or it may be a process that takes hours. In my observation, a child tends to have a fairly predictable pattern of activation and movement through a stress episode that is unique to the individual.

Close observation of the child will reveal early, subtle clues that the child's stress level is building. A good place to start is to ask the caregiver if they can spot an upset brewing, and what it is they exactly see that tells them so. During the stress episode, the clinician should pay close attention to the physiological demonstrations that the child is presenting.

Many children will present with a variety of signs, including generalized physical agitation, flat affect, flushed cheeks, pupil dilation, body rigidity, vocal changes (guttural or animal like sounds, or high pitched screams, or even complete silence). There may be hiding behaviors (under tables, desks, closets), or running away behaviors. In cases of sexual trauma history, there may be sexually precocious behavior, such as use of words and expressions uncommon to a child of a particular age.

There may be over-friendly physical expressions such as hugs and caresses that feel "creepy" to the adult. There may be spontaneous release of bladder and bowel in extreme cases. In milder cases, the child may complain of feeling ill, such as about to vomit. The point of this observation and recording of the child's specific and unique pattern of stress indicators is not only to enable highly target treatment for each behavior later on, but to become better at spotting the child's building stress, and possible longer term rhythms of symptom presentation. Understanding the particular child's particular stress tolerance and any longer term patterns of exacerbation are keys to interrupting an episode before it occurs.

In witnessing many stress episodes in children diagnosed with PTSD, perhaps the sign with the most impact on me has been the clear sense that the child is "not with me". During stress episodes, there is a clear sense the child is in a dissociative state to some degree. This effect can be quite mild and last only a few moments, or it can be very intense and last hours.

When the effect is intense, the child may demonstrate signs such as speaking gibberish to themselves, curling up in a fetal position, taking their clothes off, sexual self-stimulation, and have rapid eye darting. There is quite often an extremely flat affect and glassy eyes with pupil dilation. The important thing for the clinician to remember is that each child will have a unique, particular Stress Profile of physical reactivity behaviors.

SIGNS OF RE-EXPERIENCING

Re-experiences of a critical incident can vary in intensity and duration. Reexperiencing can range from the child recalling memories with no emotion, appropriate emotion, or all-out rage. As mentioned earlier concerning allostatic signs, children may clearly dissociate during re-experiencing events.

This can look like simple daydreaming, or be more intense with glassy eyes and extreme fear presenting. The child may also be engaged in play activities with dolls or action figures that becomes oddly intense and includes dialogs that sound decidedly grown up. If an adult tries to interrupt the re-enactment play, the child may respond as if deaf.

Re-experiencing behavioral signs can also include the child becoming panicky, running away, and hiding. If the child is recalling an assault in the past, they will essentially either defend themselves with fight or flight as they did during the assault. One small girl in my care, who was suspected of having been sexually abused by her mother's boyfriend, was playing nicely with me coloring in a coloring book, when she suddenly became quite agitated, jumped up, and threw herself on the blow-up toy clown punching bag nearby. She began to scream, "Get off me, you bastard!" and moan in a decidedly sexual manner at the same time. This spooky feeling episode (for me) illustrated a clear re-experiencing for the child, and gave me some clues that perhaps it was not she herself who had been sexually assaulted, but her mother, in her presence.

When an adult challenges PTSD children for even relatively minor misbehavior, they can be seen sometimes reacting like a deer caught in the headlights. This "freezing" effect may be accompanied by clear expressions of fear, including flinching, eye contact avoidance, or flat affect. Even when adults (such as teachers) apply the normative pressure to a child to comply with a directive or to complete schoolwork, the stress-disordered child may be triggered into a re-experience of pressure they felt during their abuse trauma.

The teacher, not understanding the child's issue, and seeing "oppositional behavior" naturally applies more pressure to the child. If the child were truly simply defiant, they would comply at some point during the pressure. But the stress-disordered child is now in a re-experience situation where they are overreacting and mistakenly reacting; they are defending themselves from perceived harm from yet another possible abuse situation.

Close observation of the child's play will also often give examples of re-experience. Play skills are often underdeveloped: there may be intolerance for individual play, parallel play quickly becomes intrusive to other children, and cooperative play is disturbed. Lack of sharing or grabbing toys may be seen. The play is likely to be at least bossy, if not aggressive and violent. Stress Disordered children spend a good bit of recess time standing in the time-out section of the playground. Play with particular toys such as dollhouses or action-figures are often excessively violent or precocious, with the child consistently undressing the dolls.

There are some theories that the play re-enactments are the efforts of the child to process their trauma. While this may be true, excessive re-enactment play may lead to behavioral problems when re-enactments with toys transition to re-enactments with other children. The clinician has a duty not only to explore and vent the violent history and attempt to heal the child from their horrible memories, but to help shape the child's play by demonstrating and engaging the child in more age normative, appropriate play.

AVOIDANCE, NUMBING AND DETACHMENT

Avoidance, numbing, and detachment in young children also follows a predictable pattern, that while paralleling adult expressions, may not be interpreted by adults correctly, or may present differently. Stress disordered children, if they are in foster care, or do not have contact with their perpetrator, will seem at times to have forgotten all about their "former" lives. In this respect, children do what adults do: they actively avoid any references to the painful past.

The difference seems to be that the child will often totally ignore and not respond at all to any mention of the past or the trauma. It is almost as if they become deaf when a person, place, or item is mentioned connected with the trauma. This effect may of course, be due in some varying part to the fact that many perpetrators give stern warnings and threats to children to keep quiet about the abuse/critical incidents.

A curious and startling effect of numbing in abused children is that they will often demonstrate a marked lack of distress or pain when injured in a way that would leave most children screaming. Sound bumps on the head, falls, and bloody skinned knees may give rise only to a momentary pause in play. On the other hand, they also may become disconsolate over very small injuries that other children would simply shake off.

Because of the physiological issues of stress, these reactions may be closely connected to the allostatic process.

If the child's body operates at a very high level of stress most of the time, their pain tolerance may be altered as if in a state of perpetual shock. This effect can be seen in combat, when soldiers are able to continue to fight in desperate situations even though they are severely wounded. The wound, at any other time agonizing, is numb for the time being.

Foster parents, in particular have noted that children diagnosed with PTSD have a high rate of variable attachment. There appears to be a wide continuum of attachment and detachment that may also have a unique pattern to the individual child. The child may be very affectionate, caring, and clingy one moment, and cold, rejecting, or totally detached the next.

This attachment and detachment continuum has implications with all of the child's relationships and potential relationships. While some children quickly become overly-familiar with strangers, other children will avoid new people with determination. The overly friendly children can be misinterpreted as simply being a friendly child, and the avoidant child as being shy. Each has a social liability. The overly friendly child may be vulnerable to re-victimization, and the avoidant child may become delayed in social isolation.

Both strategies of the children clearly have wisdom. The overly friendly child may be trying to seek adult protection (or the strategy is to try to please a potential angry perpetrator.) The avoidant child is simply trying to be very sure that the new person is safe.

The clinician may be aware that one of the diagnoses we commonly try to rule out in association with PTSD in children is Reactive Attachment Disorder (RAD). RAD is a disorder of attachment first to the primary care givers, then to others in the child's life. When a young child has experienced a chaotic family life aired with abuse, the normal attachment process can be severely disrupted. The issue with attachment disorders will be addressed further in Chapter 6.

In PTSD children with physical abuse and sexual trauma, there are quite often clear signs of varying intensity attachment problems with everyone surrounding the child. This of course, makes logical sense in that a basic task of a young child is to develop trust in others. Therefore, it may take many months to gain a valid, therapeutic working connection with a stress disordered child. Foster parents relate the same kind of problem connecting with the child, and report that it may take many months to establish even a small amount of heartfelt warmth with the child.

One sign that is startling in young children who have traumatic reactions due to abuse is lack of empathy. The average child learns empathy and expressions of caring at a very early age; one only needs to watch a two-year-old with a doll or cuddle toy. Many stress disordered children show little or no empathy for others.

PTSD children may be identified by school staff as bullying other children on the playground. In one case, a boy of age eight that I treated repeatedly grabbed the hoods of other children's coats from behind, pulling and choking them, with no apparent concern or remorse, and in fact, glee. It may very well be that their own pain tolerance is so high that they cannot recognize discomfort or pain in others very well.

Or, as in the case just mentioned, the child is passing on the negative energy and rage from their perpetrator. In the case of bullying, it is well known that abuse "slides downhill." Yet in other cases, I have seen siblings who have experienced neglect and abuse together become so empathetic and protective of each other that their egos are essentially fused.

Detachment behaviors follow low empathy quite naturally. The detachment behaviors can range from the child having a hard time in developing social and nurturing attachments to the child being so far detached at times as to be nearing *dissociation*. The sudden onset of a flat affect and dilated pupils in a stress disordered child signifies deep detachment and a concurrent allostatic process. One can see how each of the symptom categories overlap and flow into each other.

Detachment reactions, which are likely signs of a chemical "dumping" process in the child's body, can make the child highly vulnerable to successive traumas and victimization. When the child is in a detached reactive state, they may not be able to invest much cognition in protecting themselves: they may simply submit to another round of abuse.

Because of their cluster of detached, socially awkward behaviors, PTSD children will often stand out in a group of other children. Teachers may note that these children seem to be targets for other children who are bullies (even other children who are not known to be bullies). The PTSD child may gravitate towards other children who recognize them as vulnerable, and then victimize them by teasing or bullying.

These children may burn through friendships at a high rate; other children become confused by the PTSD child because one moment they are friendly and calm, the next they may be mean and highly agitated for no apparent reason. They often present a social awkwardness with peers that looks like inexperience, aggression, domination, alienation, or that they are trying far too hard to fit in. Older children with PTSD have described the feeling of being with peers as a severe "not being normal or fitting in."

RELATIONSHIP CONFUSION

The relationships, psychological alterations, and self (ego) structure of children with acute stress or post-traumatic stress will also show notable and unique damage. For some children, when they are in contact with the adult perpetrator, they will become very affectionate and regressed. These behaviors may transfer to other adult caregivers (foster parents) following contact with the perpetrator. In other children, new relationships with adults become very difficult to establish due to the child's hypervigilance concerning trust and safety.

Some stress disordered children seem to have no fear or caution around strangers, and will approach anyone with an instant-relationship hug. These children will often become very physically clingy towards substitute caregivers, such as teachers or foster parents. It is not uncommon for them to begin to call the foster parents "mommy" and "daddy" within forty-eight hours of arrival in the foster home. It is almost as if the child is so starved for physical care and comfort that they are willing to accept this from anyone. The danger of this presentation becomes obvious.

One other interesting effect that I have noted through the years is that some abused children will transfer hostility and accusations to non-perpetrating adults such as foster parents or other caregivers quite readily. I need not elaborate for the clinical reader the phenomenon of transference, but the peculiarity of a traumatic memory situation is that the child's memory may be impaired both about the details and sequence of traumatic events. The substitute caregiver is a safe person to transfer the emotional energy of the traumatic event to.

This relationship confusion may not go as far as an accusation of abuse towards a foster parent, but it may present on a day-to-day basis in the form of the child repeatedly attempting to engage the foster parent in the same fashion that the child engaged the biological parent (or perpetrator). This pattern is one that the clinician needs to be acutely aware of if the child they are treating is in foster care, and one that the clinician needs to help the foster parent cope with through specific training on how to respond to the child's negative engagement attempts.

For young children who have experienced repeated critical incidents, the world of relationships becomes a very unsatisfying, unsafe and unpredictable place. As such, the child's behaviors may be altered in reflection of this. The child begins to create their own internal safe place for their ego.

I have worked in multiple cases where the child is intensely imaginative and retreats into a self-structured internal fantasy world as a means of coping. These behaviors become so marked that concerned adults may report that the child appears not only to be severely detached from others, but to be hallucinating.

One beautiful little girl named Matilda had such a fragile ego structure when she came into care, that she would retreat into a deep fantasy state and begin to use baby talk, or sing little songs completely composed of nonsense words. The behavior would often occur prior to and following court ordered visits with her biological father. To the observer, Matilda appeared to be in a near-psychotic state. This retreat into fantasy is a reasonable defense to ego destruction via the trauma. If the external world is a very unsafe place, why not retreat to a place that feels safer?

Anyone who has witnessed a child in contact with a suspected or known perpetrator of abuse may have seen the child become very affectionate, friendly, and charming with the perpetrator. The child has structured their ego expressions to protect themselves from further abuse: if they can be pleasing to the perpetrator, perhaps the perpetrator will not abuse them again. The child's ego structure is dominated by their history of abuse, and often dominated by the perpetrator of the abuse. This effect, if repeated with other people at other times, may place the child at risk for further abuse by savvy perpetrators who instinctively seem to know how to spot such a child.

TRAUMA AND BEHAVIOR REGRESSION: A CASE STUDY

Each new trauma and each new stress episode places the child ever closer to catastrophic breakdown of their ego structure, or profound and permanent changes in their personality structure. Larger episodes of *ego decompensation* (loss of ability to maintain normal, appropriate psychological defenses, sometimes resulting in depression, anxiety or delusions) do occur during treatment, and frequently result in hospitalization. Like Matilda, children who have experienced trauma can become regressed in their behaviors when they retreat into their "safer" ego retreats. Many children I have worked with have issues with bedwetting, daytime wetting, and encopresis with feces manipulation or smearing. The following case demonstrates the connection between trauma and these kinds of behaviors.

J.T. came onto my caseload as a seven-year-old boy with mental retardation who had been age-appropriate in his toileting up until the time of his sexual abuse. J.T. lived with his mother, who was very intellectually limited and lived on the very margins of subsistence. J.T.'s mother also drank heavily at times when she became depressed. The county child protective services became involved in the case when J.T. began to push toy dinosaurs into his rectum and the mother sought help. The mother had begun to suspect that her son had been sexually abused by a male adult friend who had been babysitting the boy.

The protective services also then assessed the mother to be inadequate to care for the child. There was both neglect and physical abuse present perpetrated by the mother. Apparently, she had regularly banged the boy's head into the wall when he had misbehaved. J.T. was eventually placed in foster care, but was quickly moved from one foster home to another due to his behaviors. He eventually spent about a year in a residential treatment facility because no foster home could be found.

Following some very limited behavioral improvement, a new foster home was secured for J.T. Almost immediately, J.T. began to defecate and urinate in his bedroom, often around daybreak. He clearly had the skills to use the toilet, and could relate that he knew that the toilet was the appropriate place to put his wastes. His doctor prescribed DDAVP, but it had virtually no effect on improving the night time wetting.

Further, J.T. not only defecated in his underpants, but he began to manipulate and smear the feces on the bedclothes, walls, and himself. When asked why he did this, he simply stated: "because I want to." J.T. also made repeated statements about a ghost named "George", and frequently spoke to the ghost, with accompanying glances towards the ceiling or corners of the room.

The treatment approach was based on some spotty information from J.T. that his mother had banged his head on the wall when he had toileting accidents. J.T. also indicated that the sexual perpetrator had penetrated him anally. From this information, the theory developed that J.T. was engaging in the difficult behaviors as an anger expression. It was also noted that he may be soiling and smearing in the very early morning, leading to the theory that he may be having intrusive dreams about the abuse, subsequent strong emotions, and then the behavior. Patient and detailed questioning of J.T. revealed the ghost's name was also the name of the perpetrator.

When small children have experienced abuse at the hands of an adult, they quite naturally become full of rage. Total loss of control of one's situation and body threatens one's sense of identity at a profound level. Following the traumatic event(s), could it be that the child attempts to re-claim their ego power by finding a way to "get back at" or anger the perpetrator? Could the child be using the wetting and soiling to do this? Does the behavior have the added benefit of keeping a sexual perpetrator away from them? If the child speaks *to* the perpetrator when the perpetrator is not physically present, is it a hallucination, or a genuine ghost of powerful emotion?

J.T.'s foster parents were directed to wake earlier than J.T. to catch him before he could engage in the behaviors. They were to simply take his hand and walk to the toilet, with a non-punitive affect. When "accidents" occurred, they were to treat these as matter-of-fact, and assist J.T. in cleaning up his room and himself.

Since J.T. also greatly enjoyed taking baths, bathing was used as a reward when he used the potty. Otherwise, when he urinated or soiled in his room, he was only permitted to clean up with wet wipes. Interactive work with J.T included the exploration of George the Ghost; my chasing George away from J.T., and teaching J.T. how to change the way he spoke to George the Ghost, and how to generally stand up to George's intimidation.

J.T. showed clear progress in these areas within a few weeks, but the progress was very slow, with frequent regressions. The foster parents eventually determined that the level of care that they needed to provide for J.T. was too draining, and he was moved to another foster home, and out of my care.

I have had many other stress disordered cases of young children who have experienced the same pattern of encopresis and enuresis (inability to control the flow of urine and involuntary urination) behaviors, as well as varieties of fantasy retreat. The children range from above average to below average intelligence, and from neglect to physical and sexual abuse. In some cases, DDAVP has some limited effect for enuresis, and psychotropic medications may help with sleep and dream intrusions. In all cases, the child had gone through potty learning and had become age appropriate at some point in their toileting. I'm convinced that the enuresis and encopresis issue, as well as the marked retreat into fantasy are important behavioral markers for stress disorders associated with abuse in children.

TRAUMATIC STRESS AND MEMORY

When a person is experiencing a traumatic event, the whole of their energy is focused on self-preservation. The event itself may be so intense that the individual may need to "step out of themselves" in order to psychologically cope with the level of danger and stress. In this process, memory is often affected. In children under the age of four, developmental issues become predominant in the area of memory. At four and under, memory is not likely to be encoded verbally, but is encoded with wordless images and sensate material.

Memory in children regarding their traumatic events and the time surrounding these events often includes gaps, or "missing time" as well as difficulties in being able to sequence events accurately. Any child, let alone a traumatically stressed child, will sometimes blank out or substitute parts of a memory sequence in order to avoid embarrassment, fill in the blank for their own comfort, or in efforts to satisfy a pressing adult. This difficulty in memory sequencing seems to bleed over into everyday life for some stressed children, and this leads to further complications when adults in their life begin to accuse them of lies. Replacing a gap in one's memory with a made up "memory" that one believes to be true is called *confabulation*.

If a child was under the age of four when their abuse occurred, they will likely not be able to relate much significant material in treatment. They will also not be able to articulate very well what they are experiencing in the stress episode, or the source of their stress. They of course have the memories, but these memories are largely sensory experiences.

For example, from the time I was a small boy, I had a terrifying re-occurring dream that continued into adulthood and mystified me. I would awake with an intense physical sensation that my mouth was overfull, tongue swelled, and lips full and heavy. On the surface, this does not seem so terrifying, but it certainly was to me. As a clinician, I knew there had to be some explanation for this, but through my own self-examination, study, and even brief therapy, I could not discover it.

It was only about a year ago (at age 46) that I discovered the answer to my bad dream. In conversation with my mother, who was dying of emphysema, she (re) told me the story of my first weeks of life. I had been born on time, but was premature weight. Due to this, I was placed in an incubator for several weeks.

When my parents came to visit me, they were shocked to see that the inside of my mouth was painted a bright blue color. The hospital staff revealed to my parents that the nipples that the hospital had been using to feed the babies had been defective; they had only one very small hole in them. The nurses apparently thought that because I was so small, I was not eating very much. In fact, I was sucking so hard on the nipple, (and not getting enough food) my mouth became very sore (thus the bright blue medication swabbed in my mouth).

Though my mother had related this story to me before, it had never connected for me with my dream. But this re-telling impacted upon me like a bombshell. There no longer was any doubt for me what my dream was about. Why did it take me so long to connect the story, which I have known since I was a small boy, with the bad dream? While I do not know the answer to this deep (perhaps Freudian) mystery, I have a feeling it had something to do with my mother's impending death. Since this discovery, I have not had the dream.

At the risk of being obvious to the reader, traumatic memory does not have to be articulated verbally, it is often (perhaps more significantly) recalled through the senses. Traumatic memory, while vivid and powerful, is rarely full and robust; it is fragmented, strongly entwining discrete details with intense and terrifying emotion. Children have unique behavioral signs and symptoms of PTSD that adults do not. If the clinician, not to mention the entire treatment field, never ventures beyond the current DSM definitions and understandings of stress disorders in children, the children will not receive the quality of treatment that they deserve.

CONFUSING STRESS BEHAVIORS WITH COMMON CHILDHOOD BEHAVIORS

Often, children with Acute Stress Disorder or Post Traumatic Stress Disorder have one or more diagnoses behind them before they are accurately diagnosed with a stress disorder. Caregivers and clinicians see the behavioral signs that the child is demonstrating and come to the conclusion that the child may be ADHD, very oppositional, bi-polar, or simply under-disciplined. Though many of the behavioral signs of stress disorders are common to other disorders, when the total inventory of signs are viewed, along with any known traumatic or stressful history, the diagnosis becomes quite evident. It is also good to remember that the differences are seen in the quality, intensity, frequency, duration, as well as a known history of a trauma.

In cases where the child is living with their biological parent(s), and there is an inter-generational history of domestic abuse, addiction, or child abuse, the adults may either be in denial of the possibility of a stress disorder (or an event that has caused it), or they have become numb themselves and do not have the perspective needed to recognize the behaviors in the child as abnormal. In these cases, children are often first identified as having some kind of problem in pre-school or kindergarten.

It is amazing to me how the child is sometimes the only one who "knows" what their diagnosis is, and how adults around them (often highly educated adults) cannot figure it out. Adults, even professionals in mental health, will often not be able to "connect the dots" between demonstrated behaviors and the known history of the child's traumas. I tend to believe that many adults who work with children are so uncomfortable with the facts surrounding childhood trauma, that they unconsciously (or consciously) avoid addressing the realities of it. To be sure, it is much more comfortable to treat a child's agitated behaviors as some other diagnosis than to listen to the child describe his or her sexual abuse. Below is an overview of how each of the six behavioral sign clusters may be confused with normal childhood behaviors.

Behavioral Signs of Attempted Allostasis

Any organism under more than ordinary stress attempts to return to a balanced state called "allostasis". Various physiological and behaviors signs signal that this attempt is in process. These behavioral signs at first may be mistaken for hyperactivity or simple childhood excitement, but these signs tend to be much more intense, and not in relation to the situation around the child. The child at times seems to become very agitated, anxious, aggressive, overly shy, or very fearful for no real or apparent reason, or there appears to be an overreaction to some event or situation. This may be passed off as a sensitive or highly strung child.

The child may become very silly or overly familiar with strangers. This can be misinterpreted as the child being a "clown" or a "flirt". These children often have a very hard time calming down. There may be problems with sleep: getting to sleep, staying asleep, and nightmares. The child may startle very easily, and may be overly clingy towards caregivers. The adults in their life may label them as excitable, simply full of extra energy, or a "dynamo".

The child's appetite and bowel-bladder habits may be affected. There is often an increase in toileting accidents, intentional toileting in closets, corners, etc. The child may actually manipulate or play with their own or animal feces. There may be regressions, slow, or stalled potty learning in younger children. The adults in the child's life may label this as the child not wanting to grow up, wanting to remain a "Mamma's boy", or equate these behaviors with the child being "willful" or being "hard to break". (There may be, in fact, some truth to this, as the child may be demonstrating rage at their abuse and abuser).

Children may also express a sudden change of affect: their expression may become flat, pupils may dilate, and the child will look as if they are daydreaming, or "off in their own world". These children may be described by their parents as being a "daydreamer". Some other children may have sudden bursts of energy that look like they just had a dose of "speed", becoming very physically active and agitated very quickly. The behaviors may be passed off as simple childhood imitation of characters on TV, or a child who is "always looking for trouble".

These behavioral signs can occur at any time the child is triggered by someone, some thing, or some location in their environment. The number and kind of triggers can be difficult to ascertain, especially in younger children. Parents may have some insight into the fact that certain activities seem to get their child wound up, but cannot identify why this is so, or misidentify the reason. For example, a parent may state that his child always gets out of control when there is a visit between the child and particular cousins; in fact, it might be the perpetrating uncle of the child that is triggering the reaction. When there is a dramatic increase in agitation following contact with a person who is a trigger, this is often confused with the child being upset, sad, or disappointed that they are no longer in the person's presence or care. The key differences between a triggered PTSD episode and the child simply missing the person is that the signs are much more intense, of longer duration, and include hours if not days of severe and consistent misbehavior as well as an increase of the other five sign clusters.

Re-experiencing

These behavioral signs may be confused with a child's normal play; children may engage in violent play, sexualized play, or other re-enactments of traumatic events in their lives with action figures or dolls. This type of play may be discounted as normal due to exposure to television or friends who are a bad influence.

The child may become oppositional over small issues; they may seem to need to be in control of every situation to feel comfortable. This may be confused with being bossy, stubbornness and "being contrary". The difference is that when an average child is pressed to comply, they will give in; when a stressed child is pressed, their agitation increases to the point of getting out of control.

Children who have been sexually abused may engage in more frequent and public masturbation or simulated sex acts. They may also engage in odd behaviors, such as stuffing toilet paper or other objects in their pants. They may use explicitly sexual language, or have precocious knowledge about sex.

These behaviors are much more difficult to pass off as something else. In some cases, I have heard parents explain these behaviors as the child, once again, acting like an adult that they have seen on television, or exposure to the poor influences of the child's friends. There may be an attempt to normalize the behaviors: "all children touch themselves there", or "they are playing doctor".

Nightmares are a form of re-experiencing, but they are also quite a normal event in any child's life. The difference for stress-disordered children is the intensity and frequency of the intrusive dreams, which may be accompanied by wetting or soiling, or an inability to go back to sleep and urges to play following the dream.

Avoidance, Numbing and Detachment

This behavioral cluster can be confused with a child trying to avoid responsibilities, being stubborn, being a loner, or angry with family members. The child may actively avoid certain people, places, or items. They may seem to have forgotten all about the traumatic event that took place, or their recent acting out/stress episode. Adults can pass this off as the child having forgotten all about the traumatic event, and "being over it".

The child may not respond to every day injuries like other children; they may easily shake off scrapes and bumps without tears or any reaction at all. This is passed off as the child being "one tough little kid". On the other hand, they may become very upset and over reactive to very slight injuries, the child then being labeled "a sissy".

The child may seem to bully other children by simply ignoring the other child and "plowing on through". The child may actually physically attack another child with pinching, biting, hitting, or strangling. This may be confused with sibling rivalry or peer disagreements, but the marker is the frequency and intensity of the behaviors. They may seem to have little empathy for other people who are injured or have their feelings hurt.

In most stress-disordered children, there is often a lack of the ability to self-comfort. In play, it can also be seen that the child has not formed much attachment to any one toy; the child may not have a cuddle toy, for example. Again, this may earn the child a label of being "tough", or being a leader, or having promise for a career in professional wrestling.

Psychological Alterations

These behavioral signs may be confused with a child who is "spoiled". The child may continue to try to sleep in the caregiver's bed, they may show regressed developmental behaviors, such as daytime wetting, using "baby talk", or a desire to use a pacifier or bottle, or becoming very clingy to the caregiver. The child may exhibit memory problems or confabulate wild stories or fantasies that are considerably more detailed or odd than the average child's active imagination.

The child may become hypervigilant; they may be very watchful and seem anxious, or fearful of being abandoned. Parents of these children will often either ridicule the child for their regressed behaviors, or indulge the behaviors, keeping the child "their baby" or protecting them as extraordinarily fragile. The child and their parents may demonstrate odd or altered views of the world and society that they proudly legitimize as "being different" than other people, or being a "born rebel". There may be a kind of fatalism and resignation presented by the child and family.

The child may be very impulsive, and engage in risky play without apparent understanding of the danger. The child may either have gained a very hostile and negative attitude towards the world, or they present themselves to others as very vulnerable, and then get taken advantage of or are re-victimized. The adults in the child's life may call them a "daredevil", or in the latter case, support them vehemently as victims of a hostile world (teachers, counselors, and police).

Relational Problems

This set of behavioral signs may be confused with an over shyness, or a child who "has not had the right discipline", or is "full of themselves". The child may have trouble trusting others, may be secretive and very guarded. The child may have problems making and keeping friends.

They may "try too hard" to be friendly or to fit in. The child may become very bossy and parentified. There may physical boundary problems in the way the child relates to others, such as standing too close, touching too freely or too soon in a relationship. The child may touch others inappropriately, such as tickling or sexualized touching. The child may seem to crave help, care, and affection, but when it is given, push the helper away.

These children will often be quickly identified as behavior problems when they start school. Quite often, the family is so used to these aberrations, and other family members exhibit similar behaviors, making them normalized in the family.

Ego Structure

These behavioral signs may be confused with a child who is simply "down" or depressed. The child may seem to be very emotionally fragile and "fall apart" easily. Again, this may be passed off as a "sensitive child". They may verbalize low self-esteem, or blame themselves for the bad things that have happened to them.

The parents may identify and defend their child as a victim of other children's (or teachers, counselors, etc.) hostility. The child may alternate from being very oppositional and defensive to being excessively cooperative and easily led. The adults surrounding the child may explain this as the child being "a fighter", or alternately, a child who "just wants to make friends."

There may be periods of time where the child retreats into extraordinarily detailed fantasy. They may even have their own secret language and/or have different names for themselves. While other children and adults may find this to be odd, the parents of the child may find this "charming" and marvel at the child's "wild imagination" or be amused at their "imaginary friend".

Essentially, the markers for a child with a stress disorder as opposed to normal childhood behaviors becomes: known critical incidents, the presence of all six clusters of behavioral signs, the intensity of the signs above average childhood behaviors, and the duration, and frequency at which they occur.

Chapter 4

National Association for People Abused in Childhood (NAPAC)

Lucy Duckworth, Communications and Outreach Officer at the National Association for People Abused in Childhood (NAPAC) gives an insight into how child abuse affects our whole society and the services adult survivors of childhood abuse can expect

Lucy Duckworth

THE PROBLEM

Childhood abuse is perhaps one of the most controversial and 'taboo' subjects in society today. This alone is quite confusing, as, apart from abusers, the majority of society condemns such acts. There is no worse crime; no crime that leaves a longer legacy and no crime that has such a huge ripple effect on society. So why do we simply not want to know?

Perhaps, because we will have to admit that, as adults, we continually fail children? Because we will have to face the fact that people we know and love are capable of such evil crimes? That if we truly face the scale of the problem, we may have to ask, 'will we ever have trust in people or society again?' Is there hope of eradicating this nasty crime? Giving survivors the opportunity to speak out will go some way to doing that. The guilt for families of survivors is often so bad that the families themselves don't want to talk about it, are unable to support the survivor, sometimes blaming the family member who was the victim. This often makes them feel alone, as they would have felt when they were being abused and reinforcing the false belief that somehow it was their fault. Supporting a survivor is very challenging and, for families, can often be intertwined with feelings of guilt and blame. All these negative feelings belong with the abuser, but for families and survivors, letting go of them often takes many years, if ever achieved.

Abusers are adept at passing the responsibility for their crime to their victims and their families. We must not forget to provide support to the families of victims so that they can be part of the healing process.

NAPAC is often contacted by many family members or those caring for survivors and very often they just don't know what to say or do. All society needs to be educated and stay informed about the devastating and lifelong consequences of abuse. As you can see below, the consequences affect us all, and to people who say "I've never met an abuse survivor" we say "yes you have, you just didn't know it".

HOW IT AFFECTS US ALL

Most of society's problems have their roots in childhood abuse, for example: eating disorders; obesity; homelessness; depression; criminality (over 70% of people in prison are survivors of childhood abuse); self mutilation; alcoholism and drug addiction; and suicide, to name but a few. It is a proven fact that we could reduce crime, improve healthcare and improve education by simply reducing childhood abuse.

What about the survivors that do grow up and finally, well into their adulthood, decide they need to get help and face the past? Pastoral care for survivors and their families is patchy to say the least. Few would argue that six counselling sessions courtesy of the NHS is not going to even scratch the surface. Worse still, scratching the surface can be even more damaging to the individual if on-going support is not available. Opening that can of worms can have devastating consequences if proper support is not there for the individual. Support groups run by untrained people, assessments by a variety of psychiatrists, each offering different agendas and advice, (as many survivors have to go

through to provide evidence for their criminal case) can be extremely damaging. Survivors must 'heal at their own pace'. Pushing expectations above capability can be very dangerous for long term health, and often evoke a sense of failure. It is essential to remember that as adults, the scale of damage varies from person to person, but it is often enduring and lifelong.

There are five types of childhood abuse: neglect, sexual, physical, emotional and ritual. Some people fail to recognise the latter but we know from listening to many victims that it exists. Some cultures excuse abuse as they say it is part of their belief system—child witchcraft, genital mutilation, child marriages and abuse carried out in groups, perhaps with religious artefacts. Many of these categories overlap; it goes without saying that emotional abuse is suffered by all victims of any of the other four categories. However, emotional abuse standing alone is all too common, where children are constantly told negative things and deprived of a stable emotional relationship. What we must remember is that all abuse is harmful. It is an unwanted invasion of a child's space, body and spirit. It is an alteration of a developing personality and a destabilising, shattering of an innocent childhood.

At NAPAC, we don't like to categorise abuse. To do so is bad news for the victim and for society as a whole. No one but the victim can say how it has affected him or her. Every month hundreds of people tell us about the devastation it has caused them. We never say "we know how you feel" or even pretend to. Even though most of us at NAPAC are survivors ourselves, abuse is so personal, we can understand but we cannot know how the survivor feels. But just offering this understanding is helpful for survivors, and a unique service not provided anywhere else.

WHAT NOW?

NAPAC is the only UK national charity that supports adult survivors of all forms of childhood abuse. Founded in 1997, NAPAC runs Britain's only 'Helplines Association' accredited free phone support line for adult survivors. In 1997 the founder of NAPAC discovered that the only place survivors had to turn to was ChildLine. And of course, ChildLine is for children. Now part of NSPCC, ChildLine needed somewhere to refer adult survivors and thus was instrumental in helping to get NAPAC started. The NAPAC Support Line is staffed entirely by volunteers some of whom are survivors themselves. Unlike many charities, we get no government funding although we have been fortunate to have obtained a successful grant from the Big Lottery Fund. This lack of government funding is despite the fact that setting up NAPAC was a key recommendation of the National Commission of Inquiry into the Prevention of Child Abuse.[1] Research shows that the average time it takes a survivor to disclose the abuse they suffered is 22 years after it ended. Callers to our Support Line appear to confirm this as many are well into their 40's, 50's and 60's and have never before spoken of the abuse. So NAPAC is clearly not a service that should be marginalised. It is an essential life-saver.

Much of the feedback we receive confirms this. We are also increasingly hearing from younger survivors who are thankfully getting help earlier. Early intervention and support is vital if these young people are to grow and lead fulfilled lives. A vitally important recommendation of the National Commission stated that giving adult survivors a voice was essential to child protection. We reply to every letter or e-mail, we offer accredited training in how to

> Research shows that the average time it takes a survivor to disclose the abuse they suffered is 22 years after it ended.

work with survivors and resources permitting, are currently rolling this programme out across social services, GP's, prisons and other institutions where abuse is sadly still rife. We send out information packs to survivors and for those looking for one to one or group support we explore all the possibilities.

As a charity NAPAC is certainly unique. No other organization does what we do. But supporting adult survivors is not a 'cosy cause'. It stands to reason that if society has difficulties in addressing the issue of child abuse then helping those children when they have grown up will be even more problematic. And of course, because abuse knows absolutely no socioeconomic, ethnic or cultural boundaries it stands to reason that there are many highly intelligent, influential and powerful abusers in society and they do not want their crimes spoken of. They do not want NAPAC to exist. But we do because we have to. And we are growing every day. The only way to help the millions of adult survivors of abuse and to protect our children today is to stay informed and start talking about a subject we would all like to ignore; it is a moral duty that every person in society must share.

For more information about NAPAC's Services and how to support us, go to www.napac.org.uk

Lucy Duckworth
Communication and Outreach Consultant,
lucy@napac.org.uk

REFERENCE

1. Childhood matters: Report of the National Commission of Inquiry into the Prevention of Child Abuse, HMSO, London, 1996

Child Abuse and Neglect

Thomas W. Roberts

CHAPTER 5 PRETEST (T/F)

1. Researchers have found that neglect is a greater factor in abused children's reduced language acquisition than other forms of abuse.
2. According to research, a child's probability of being raped is approximately three times the probability of that of an adult.
3. When compared to all reported sexual assault, child sexual assault accounts for more than two-thirds of all cases.
4. The majority of sex crimes are committed by persons who are excited by and seek out children for sexual gratification.
5. Accidental disclosure is the most common way sexual abuse of young children is discovered.
6. All sexual abuse cases involve being touched.
7. Researchers have found that PTSD resulting from sexual abuse affects the same gene activity as PTSD from other traumatic experiences.
8. Overall, sexual abuse within the family is considered rare.
9. Researchers have found that abuse is less reported by both female and male victims.
10. Sending sexually explicit content over social media could result in being charged as a sexual predator.

CHILD ABUSE AND NEGLECT

Child abuse and neglect is defined by both the federal government and by state laws for both criminal and civil purposes. Child Abuse and Prevention and Treatment Act (CAPTA) (2010) defines abuse as "any recent act or failure to act on the part of a parent or caretaker, which results in death, serious physical or emotional harm, sexual abuse or exploitation, or an act or failure to act which presents an imminent risk of serious harm," (p. 1). Neglect is sometimes categorized separately and refers to a host of parental behaviors in which proper attention is not given to the child leading to child endangerment. Behaviors range from not providing for health concerns of the child to tacit allowance of the child's use of drugs and alcohol. Laws regarding child abuse and neglect are applied to parents or immediate caregivers, but not to nonfamily members who are not occupying a position of caregiver. The rate of child abuse and neglect of substantiated cased in California in 2012 was 8.9 per 1,000 (Needell et al., 2012). Child abuse and neglect are categorized into four types, including physical, neglect, sexual, and emotional abuse (Giovannoni and Becerra, 1979). These types may be broadened to include abandonment or, in some cases, neglect because of the substance abuse of the parent. These categories are not mutually exclusive and overlapping occurs.

Child abuse and neglect is a major problem for children in the United States. Estimates are that more than 3.3 million children are abused in the U.S. every year, the highest number of abuse among industrialized nations. Children of all races and ethnic backgrounds are represented as victims of abuse and neglect, but some differences are noted. The number of children who die from abuse has increased over the past 15 years and now stands at approximately 2,000 per year (U.S. Department of Health and Human Services, 2011). The alarming fact is that the majority of child deaths because of abuse occur to children younger than four years of age. In addition, many children die from abuse that is not given as an official cause of death. The probability of severe injury and death from child abuse increases dramatically, perhaps as much as 50 times, when children are raised in non-biological homes (Schnizer and Ewigman, 2005). Abuse tends to continue across generations since approximately 30% of children who were abused as children later abuse their own children. Not only is abuse of children physically and emotionally damaging to children but it is also an economic burden on society, with an annual cost of about 125 billion dollars a year (Fang, Brown, Florence, and Mercy 2012).

The U.S. was slow to protect children from abuse and only after public outcry over the beating of a child by foster parents in 1875 was a law enacted to protect children. It was not until the 1960s that states took child abuse seriously and enacted laws to further protect children (Myers, 2008). This surge of attention to the plight of children followed the publication on child abuse that coined the phrase **battered child syndrome**. Pediatric radiologists became important in identifying severe abuse resulting from the parent shaking the child and causing neurological damage, such as subdural hematoma, retina hemorrhage, and cerebral edema.

TABLE 5.1 Frequency of abuse and neglect (From American Humane Society http://www.ameri-canhumane.org/children/stop-child-abuse/fact-sheets/child-abuse-and-neglect-statistics.html)

Neglect	62.8%
Physical abuse	16.6%
Sexual abuse	9.3%
Emotional/psychological abuse	7.1%
Medical neglect	2.0%
Other	14.3%

In recent years much has been written about the decline in the number of substantiated child abuse and neglect cases. A number of factors contribute to the decline in the overall number of cases, including a focus on prevention and treatment, rapid response to missing children reports, and neighborhood notification programs. According to Finkelhor and Jones (2004), it is necessary to identify the reason for the lower numbers because otherwise there may be a false impression of the safety of children in U.S. society, given the fact that the U.S. rate is higher than other industrialized nations.

One possible reason for the decline in child abuse and neglect cases investigated by Finkelhor and Jones (20004) was reporting standards by Child Protective Services (CPS). They reviewed state reports on substantiated cases to determine if CPS standards were more conservative, that is, not labeling some cases of abuse that had been labeled as such in the past. Their investigation found that a survey of all states revealed that the same percentage of substantiated cases was reported annually, with no evidence that a more conservative labeling of abuse occurred.

Finkelhor and Jones (2004) concluded that there was more than likely a decline in the number of cases because of a drop in the number of sexual abuse cases. They point out the decline in crime rates for the period and improved home environments for children. It would be expected that as the home environment improves, the well-being of children would also improve. The decline in sexual abuse of children is also represented by the amount of focus and attention given to this form of maltreatment. When rates decrease there is support for the social policies that led to the decrease. Policymakers feel encouraged that their efforts were rewarded and continue in the effort to further reduce occurrences. Further concerns regarding reporting of abuse should address the differences in the collecting and sharing of data from CPS and law enforcement agencies. Data from CPS tend to be gathered inconsistently across districts, which become somewhat problematic in complying and making sense of the data.

PHYSICAL ABUSE

Physical abuse is damage to the child inflicted by the parent or caregiver that causes physical injury. Whether the parent intended to damage the child is irrelevant. A wide range of parental behaviors can result in injury to the child. Most often the parent tries to discipline the child and takes measures that cause the injury, which can range from a mild bruise to broken bones and even death.

Spanking (Corporal Punishment)

The method of **spanking (corporal punishment)** as a type of discipline has been highly correlated with abuse, although spanking as such is not considered abusive. Since spanking involves hitting a child, there can be a fine line between appropriate spanking and abuse. While few experts in child and family development or therapists who work clinically with child problems and parenting promote spanking as a means of discipline, the vast majority of parents admit to spanking their children, especially young children (Straus, 2000). Research on spanking reveals that children can be affected beyond any physical injury they may receive. Physical punishment of a child is one of the oldest parental means of discipline and a way to gain control of the child's annoying behavior. Recent studies show that there are long-term negative effects of being spanked, but no research shows long-term positive effects (Walton, 2012). One of the most common effects is **depression,** which can be a lifelong condition. Of major concern is that children learn from being spanked that aggression gives advantages, and solving problems most notably can be accomplished through aggressive means. Perhaps the most damaging effect is the damage to the parent/child relationship. Children are not as trusting or bonded to parents who spank them. Children may resent parents for spanking them, but seemingly are unaffected in other ways. However, the long-term effects are less supportive to helpful relationships with parents, siblings, coworkers, and partners.

New brain imaging research bolsters older research that found negative outcomes from physical abuse. For example, researchers have found that children who are abused physically have reduced gray matter and slightly lower IQs. Their brains also produce lower amounts of dopamine similarly to persons with addiction disorders, and they are prone to depression, anxiety disorders, substance abuse and alcoholism, and, to some degree, suicidal ideation throughout the lifespan. A recent study found that the association between mental illness and being spanked as a child is significant, accounting for from 2% to 7% of mental illness, including depression, and **mood disorders** and **anxiety disorders** (Afifi, Mota, Dasiewicz, MacMillan, and Sareen, 2012). Afifi and associates focused on less severe physical punishment such as non-abusive spanking in a large national sample of subjects in the U.S.

Not everyone agrees that non-abusive spanking is related to mental disorders in children and have lifelong consequences. For example, Robert Larzelere and Brett Kuhn (2005) reviewed 26 research studies on non-abusive spanking and found that physical punishment was only negative when it was the only form of punishment or not applied appropriately. Larzelere and Kuhn contend that appropriate non-abusive spanking following noncompliant behavior to other disciplinary tactics includes one or two swats across the buttocks with an open hand followed by the parent, whose emotions are under control, providing an explanation for the spanking and assuring the child of the parent's love. They refer to this type of spanking as **conditional spanking,** which they believe does not damage the child emotionally. Furthermore, Larzelere and Kuhn believe that all forms of disciplinary actions of the parent are related to later behavioral misconduct and, in this regard, spanking is no different than other methods. In addition, they believe that comparing children who were spanked against children who were not spanked, and perhaps did not need parental intervention, is comparing apples and oranges. Instead researchers should only compare children who need disciplinary intervention. They found that there is no difference in outcomes between other forms of discipline and spanking when an intervention was needed by the parents. While Larzelere and Kuhn raise interesting questions, those who oppose spanking would question how many parents actually use conditional spanking and would point out that the majority of child abuse occurs when parents are disciplining a child. Opponents believe that few parents use spanking when they are not angry and few rationally explain the reason for the spanking to their child.

Beaten or Hit with Objects Causing Physical Damage

Physical abuse causing bodily harm results from being hit, grabbed, slapped, shaken, pushed, hit with an object, and other similar parental behaviors. While children from all types of backgrounds can be physically abused, the probability is greater in certain types of families. Families in poverty with low levels of education, families with mothers who smoke, single-parent families, and children born with low birth weights all predict higher rates of abuse (Schnitzer and Ewigman, 2005). In addition, disabled children have an increased probability of being abused.

Most experts believe that physical abuse is underreported because definitions and reporting of abuse vary (Panel on Research on Child Abuse and Neglect, 1993). Underreported cases of child abuse fit a particular profile, which includes being White, living with parents, young in age rather than adolescent, and having head or stomach injuries. In underreported cases of head or stomach injuries, children are more likely to die from their injuries than those with similar injuries from accidental causes. Generally, the probability of being abused increases with age, but the more severe abuse occurs with young children.

As mentioned above, abusive behavior toward the child affects the growth of gray matter in the developing brain. Brain imaging shows that gray matter increases from early childhood until about age 10 when **pruning** and **myelination** occur (Sowell et al., 2003). Stress and trauma such as from parental abuse can cause a disruption in the brain development of the child through specific brain systems including the **hypothalamic-pituitary-adrenal (HPA) axis, sympathetic nervous system (SNS),** and **serotonin** (Watts-English, Fortson, Gibler, Hooper, and DeBellis, 2006). Long-term emotional responses and the formation of memory and learning are heavily influenced by these three brain systems. While IQ differences of abused children compared with children who were not abused have been found, some studies have found no differences (Pollak et al., 2010). In adults, research has not demonstrated a significance difference in IQ scores based on being abused as a child. Numerous studies have investigated the relationship of abuse and memory impairment with mixed results. Most studies on the cognitive outcomes of physical abuse do not control for co-existing morbidities, which means that the results of poor cognitive effects, including learning and memory, may be caused by other factors (Navalta, Polcari, Webster, Boghossian, and Teicher, (2006). It is likely that memory impairment is found only with a concomitant circumstance of **Post-Traumatic Stress Disorder (PTSD)** (Samuelson, Krueger, Burnett, and Wilson, 2010). In addition, a number of studies have reported that visual and attention issues are related to physical abuse and neglect, but the studies fail to control for confounded variables.

A large number of studies have investigated emotional processing in children who have been physically abused or neglected. These findings suggest that children who were physically abused or neglected tend to react to anger directed at them and to recognize angry facial expressions, while their recognition of other emotional expressions is blunted (Fries and Pollak, 2004). Research shows that emotional processing of abused and neglected children is less adequate in childhood, but the deficits disappear by adulthood (Ochsner and Gross, 2005).

Signs of Physical Child Abuse

Physical child abuse usually leaves bruises in areas of the body not normally bruised in play, including the face, head, buttocks, and abdomen. Injury to these parts of the body can cause severe damage, such as retinal detachment, swelling and blood hemorrhage in the brain, and broken bones. Other telltale signs of child abuse can be the found by analyzing the bruise. Frequently, the shape of an object used by the parent can be found on the child's body, such as the imprint of a belt or hand. Sometimes the injury is not apparent during visual inspection, but nevertheless, can be just a severe as a noticeable injury. Because physical injury is common in children, and, at times, unusual accidental injury may resemble abusive injuries, persons interacting with the child may be ambivalent about the cause of the injury. Consequently, a thorough investigation beginning with the child's past and present behaviors can help clarify an accurate understanding of the reasons for the injuries (Springer, Sheridan, Kuo, and Carnes, 2007).

In some cases it is difficult to determine the age or reason for the injury, such as denture marks or burns. Some children of abuse have bite marks on various parts of their bodies, usually hidden by clothing. Adult bite marks can be distinguished from child bite marks by size (Wagner, 1986). Burn marks are difficult to determine from natural injury. However, burns resulting from parental or caretaker action tend to differ from accidental burns, which may occur on extremities such as arms or legs and are more likely to be from hot liquid spills or touching hot objects.

One of the most serious injuries from abuse is to the head, which is related to **subdural and retina hemorrhages**. Head injuries are frequently correlated with hospital treatment, either as an emergency room visit or hospitalization, and are more likely to lead to death than other types of injuries (Reece and Sege, 2000). Head injury, such as skull fracture, can occur from any cause including accidental falls. Because children with head injuries may be asymptomatic, many injuries may go unnoticed. Retina hemorrhages, which may also go unnoticed and untreated, can be distinguished by general pattern from accidental injury.

TABLE 5.2   Symptoms of physical abuse

Physical Symptoms of Child Abuse Include:
1. Black eyes and facial bruises
2. Broken bones that would appear to be non-accidental
3. Bruise marks in the shapes of objects or fingers
4. Bruises in unusual places
5. Damage to the head
6. Burns that differ from splashes
7. Choke marks on the neck
8. Cigarette burns
9. Marks around the wrists or ankles
10. Bite marks
11. Whelp marks

In addition to physical signs of abuse, the abused child may show behavioral changes in mood, compliance, and emotionality. The child's regular routines of play, interacting with others, and alone time may be disrupted. The child may attempt to avoid being home and make excuses to be with friends. Although child physical abuse occurs from many reasons, it can be related to parents' unrealistic expectations of their child and demanding responses from the child that are beyond his/her developmental level. Children sometimes speak of odd or eccentric parental behavior to classmates and teachers, which can be a sign of domestic instability often associated with abuse. Descriptions of parental behavior by the child at school or with friends that indicate mood swings or erratic decision-making may also indicate that a parent is mentally ill or a substance abuser. Vague, nondescript, and various explanations for the injury given by the child or caregiver are other red flags that abuse may have occurred. Children who are physically abused may have absences from school and be withdrawn and preoccupied when at school. They may not have appropriate peer interactions, exhibiting either withdrawn or aggressive behavior. They may also show signs of restlessness and anxiety, mimicking symptoms of ADHD. While these descriptions alone do not represent abuse, coupled with other indicators they should not be summarily ignored or dismissed.

NEGLECTED CHILDREN

Neglected children also have distinct behavioral, psychological and physical characteristics that distinguish them from non-neglected children. It is not uncommon that neglected children may have vitamin deficiencies, tooth decay, and worn or poorly sized clothing. They tend to be chronically hungry and lack attention to proper hygiene. They are fatigued from poor nutrition and tend to lack energy to complete tasks. They typically lack adult supervision and are exposed to dangerous situations. While these conditions may emanate from other causes, care must be given to determine if neglect is implicated.

Child neglect is the most frequent form of child maltreatment accounting for approximately two-thirds of referral cases and the most ignored in the literature (Wilson and Horner, 2004). Scholarly articles and theory development on neglect and the effects on children are ignored in both popular media and academic publications. The paucity of literature may be due to the nature of neglect or the ignoring of the needs of the child, which can be difficult to identify objectively. This much is known, however, that the youngest children are the most victimized. Neglect is deeply rooted in parenting behaviors typical of mentally ill or substance-abusing parents. Neglect is viewed as a chronic parental behavior that reoccurs often. Parents are engaged in a chronic pattern of inadequate protection and supervision of their children. Families that lack two parents, have work schedules that leave children alone for hours at a time, and fail to provide effective discipline at times when they do interact with their children are more likely to have neglected children. The single stressed-out mother is the poster child for what neglect looks like, although families of all backgrounds can be guilty of neglect. While the main focus of neglect is on the mother, little is written about father absence on neglect. These families tend to be poor and live in undesirable neighborhoods. Families in which neglect is usually found have multiple problems and tend to need public support on a variety of fronts. Addressing the parenting issue of failure to protect the child is only one method of intervention.

Also included in neglect is allowing the child to participate in dangerous activities that defy common sense. For example, parents involved in the use and distribution of drugs may inadvertently provide the opportunities for the child to engage in such activities. While the parent may not directly encourage the child in these harmful and illicit activities, the fact that they are not protected from engaging in them is neglectful. Whether the parent actually intends the neglectful behavior is a moot point because the negative consequences for the children would be the same. Ultimately, neglect is viewed as any behavior on the part of the parent that abnegates the parenting role and requires that the child make decisions or engage in activities that may be beyond his or her developmental level (Wilson and Horner, 2004).

One of the ways parents of neglected children have been described is as demoralized, or a kind of numbness and a giving up of effort to make things better (Wilson and Horner, 2004). This moral apathy has is roots in alcohol and drug addiction as well as abject poverty. Parents with a combined income of less than $15,000 a year are 44 times more likely to neglect their children when compared to parents making more than $30,000 a year. Neglecting parents abuse alcohol and drugs for different reasons, but regardless of the reason, the connection of substance abuse to neglect of children is strong. Some parents may be antisocial, while others may abuse alcohol and drugs as a coping mechanism for mental illness. When parents are impaired for whatever reason, they do not provide adequate supervision or attention to children.

Not all neglecting parents, however, are impaired through alcohol or drug use or are mentally ill. Some are preoccupied with jobs or other activities and spend little time interacting with their children. While **dual-career couples**, defined as both parents invested in career development and advancement and receiving a great deal of satisfaction and personal fulfillment from their jobs, may provide for the physical and material needs of their children, they could be at risk for neglecting their children's need for interaction and emotional support. Busy parents may lack the time and energy to engage their children in mutual activities. These cases typically would not be reported to child protective services and would not be included in statistical reports. Neglect in affluent families takes a decidedly different route than neglect in poor families, yet the outcomes on children may be similar. In affluent families child care is usually accomplished through hired nannies or private child care. While it cannot be argued that the use of child care professionals is in any way neglectful, depending on the circumstances, spending little time with a parent and the majority of time with paid care may raise the risk attachment disorder (Belsky, 1986).

Other underlying factors in child neglect are children exposed to domestic violence and children who live in neighborhoods in which there is an elevated concern for one's safety and security. Families in which **domestic violence** is a frequent occurrence may be at greater risk for neglect of children. Typically, when the mother is in an abusive relationship there tends to be a concomitant failure to protect children who are either abused or neglected themselves (Radford and Hester, 2006).

While neglect is often associated with the postbirth environment, there is substantial evidence that the prenatal period can be characterized by neglect. For example, pregnant women who do not provide for a positive **prenatal environment** free of alcohol or smoke exposure are either intentionally or non-intentionally neglectful of their children. Typically, a woman's behavior toward the care and needs of her child before birth parallels behavior after the birth. [...]

EFFECTS OF NEGLECT ON THE CHILD

While there is little focus on child neglect, it is well established that neglect has a profound effect on children. Researchers have found that infancy and early childhood are particularly vulnerable time periods (Hildyard and Wolfe, 2002). For infants, neglect may affect the development of attachment as measured by the Bayley Scales of Infant Development. Children of neglect may also have cognitive deficits and memory problems. Emotional neglect, in which parents fail to provide for basic psychological support, is more difficult to detect because there are no physical evidence or standout behaviors that prick the attention of others. The **failure to thrive syndrome,** in which infants fail to develop according age expectations, results from the lack of warm and supportive contact with caregivers.

FIGURE 5.1   Neglected child. Copyright © 2012 Depositphotos/olesiabilkei

Research on neglect consistently finds that children have anxious attachment with their parents, which develops very early and is pervasive throughout life. Generally, the effects of abuse rest on several factors including the age of the child at the time of the neglect, factors that are considered protective, the duration and severity of the neglect, and the quality of the parent/child relationship. One of the major causes of reduced brain growth is inadequate nutrition, resulting in cognitive and language delays. For children zero to three, there is a need for repeated language to develop vocabulary. When the caregiver ignores the babbling and other vocal attempts to get the caregivers attention, development of language will be delayed. Studies have found that neglect is a greater factor in reduced language acquisition than other forms of abuse (Gaudin, 1993).

Emotional effects of neglect are correlated with distant and distrustful relationships with parent caregivers. This lack of trust in intimate relationships may also be related to the inability to understand the emotions of others and to lack empathy. Neglected children may lack both confidence in their social ability and have reduced capacity for understanding the feelings of others. They may appear apathetic in situations in which others have very strong emotions. Their responsiveness to emotional input may be shallow and inappropriate, resulting in poor peer relationships. Low self-esteem, juvenile delinquency, drug and alcohol abuse and addiction, and poor academic achievement are other noted outcomes of neglect (Goldman, Salus, Wolcott, and Kennedy, 2003). Children who experience neglect often are described as having **global neglect**, or deficits in a number of spheres. Global neglect is related to smaller brain growth in young children, which affects brain size. While these effects appear and are noticeable early in development, the negative effects persist throughout the lifespan.

3-Year-Old Children

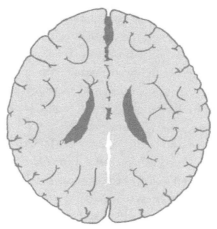

Normal

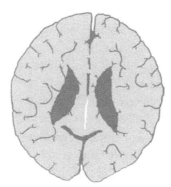

Extreme Neglect

FIGURE 5.2   Brain image of severe neglect (Bruce Perry Child Trauma Academy https://childtrauma.
org/wp-content/uploads/2013/11/McCainLecture_Perry.pdf)

Neglect is also felt on a societal level as economic risks. Neglect of a young child is highly correlated with later juvenile delinquency, adult crime, mental and emotional illness, substance abuse, and domestic violence. Furthermore, the inability to maintain steady employment in adulthood may be a long-term effect of neglect. The economic cost of treatment over the lifespan of children of neglect is far greater than the cost of prevention (Greder and Brotherson, 2001).

Risk Factors

While neglect occurs across the family demographic board, some families experience more risk for neglect than others. As risk factors increase, the probability of neglect will increase, especially if there is a decrease in protective factors. Many children live in an environment, such as poor, unsafe, and overcrowded neighborhoods, that contributes to neglect. Living in unsafe and dangerous neighborhoods is related to a host other risk factors, such as poor nutrition, exposure to lead, lack of outdoor activities, and gang infestation. While no single risk factor is the cause of neglect, the greater the accumulating of factors, the higher the probability of neglect (Ernst, Meyer, and DePanfilis, 2004). Although a poor environment is highly correlated with neglect, when many protection factors are present, such as strong parent-child relationships, positive and supportive marital partners, and community support, these families can function at a high level.

Family variables related to neglect include the presence of domestic violence (Kantor and Little, 2003). Victims of domestic violence may also lack the ability to protect the child from being abused and neglected, often referred to as the **failure to protect**. Research indicates that children are well aware of the domestic violence even when parents think otherwise (Bragg, 2003). Family stress, particularly referred to as **chronic stress**, subjects parents to on-going anxiety and fear, which is then acted out in their role relationships. This includes the parent/child relationship, which results in reduced parenting efficiency. Families experiencing chronic stress have less ability to respond appropriately to stress than other families, and even minor unexpected events can cause maladaptive responses.

Family variables, including positive and open communication patterns, the expression of empathy, and problem solving ability combine to reduce the probability of neglect. Families with active and engaged fathers, regardless of the environment in which the family lives, tends to produce better overall outcomes in children and be a protective factor against neglect (Corcoran and Nichols-Casebolt, 2004). These positive relationship skills enhance cohesion and family emotional bonding.

Characteristics of parents are important variables in the risk for neglect. For example, parents with mental or emotional problems fit a general profile for greater risk for neglecting their children. In addition, parents who were themselves abused as children and were reared in unstable and chaotic families are more likely to neglect their children (Tolan, Sherrod, Gorman-Smith, and Henry, 2004). Parents who had problems with their parents and had histories of running away or removal from the home and placed in foster care have higher incidences of neglect and abuse as adults. This connection to the parent's past issues is reflected in all types of abuse and neglect.

Other factors involving parents who contribute to neglect include substance abuse, the age and gender of the parent, and past arrests by the police. Women are more likely to neglect children, especially young poorly educated mothers (Stowman and Donahue, 2004). Research studies have found that parents who abuse substances are more likely to engage in all forms of child abuse and neglect (Kelley, 2002).

Young children, children with special needs, and children with behavioral problems are the most likely to be neglected. Children with special needs require more attention and parental support than other children, which may result in increasing the parents' stress and anxiety. This can result in neglectful behaviors that are meant to restore the parents' emotional equilibrium (Goldman, Salus, Wolcott, and Kennedy, 2003).

Prevention and treatment can be aimed at the child, the parents, or the family. Because families who abuse their children have multiple problems, a family approach to both prevention and treatment may be the most effective. A systems paradigm in which behaviors of individual members are viewed as mutually caused and maintained, provides a comprehensive model for reducing the number of abuse and neglect cases and simultaneously treating such families. Family therapy based on systems theory has a long clinical history of addressing dysfunctional families. On-going treatment and support, which takes place in the perpetrator's home, has been found to be an effective strategy (Thomlison, 2004).

CHILD SEXUAL ABUSE

Sexual abuse of children is broadly defined as any act or threat of act of sexual aggression toward a child where there is an age differential, regardless of whether the child gives consent. Incidences of sexual abuse are difficult to determine because many cases are reported some time after the abuse occurs. According to research, as much as 75% of child sexual abuse is not reported until after at least a year (Broman-Fulks et al, 2007). According to the Centers for Disease Control (CDC) (20014), approximately 25% of girls and 16% of boys are sexually victimized before the age of 18. According to research, a child's probability of being raped is approximately three times the probability that an adult will be raped. When compared to all reported sexual assaults, child sexual assault accounts for more than two-thirds of all cases. When survey data of incidences of child sexual abuse are compared, there is little consistency in findings; this suggests that a major hurdle in understanding the extent of child sexual abuse is disparate methods of collecting data (Gardner, 1989). Increased reporting of child sexual abuse has increased in the U.S. because of mandatory reporting by professionals who come in contact with families and children. Currently, approximately 10% of reported cases of child abuse and neglect are child sexual abuse.

Contrary to popular belief, the majority of child sexual abuse cases are not committed by pedophiles, or persons who are sexually excited by and seek out children for sexual gratification. Male juveniles account for approximately 36% of cases of sexual victimization (Crimes Against Children Research Center, UNH, 2010). In addition, most cases of rapes are committed by an acquaintance, friend of the family, or family member. Researchers have found a link between sexual perpetrators of adults and perpetrators of children. For example, researchers, using a polygraph methodology in interviewing sexual offenders, found that more than 80% of child sexual abusers also raped adult females and, conversely, at least one-half of those found guilty of raping adults had also sexually abused children.

Reporting of child abuse varies, which, to some degree, accounts for inconsistencies in the finding. For example, researchers using clinical samples tend to conclude that there are higher familial sexual abuse cases than for researchers using non-clinical samples. Differences in gender of children who are sexually abused have generally been found by researchers. In addition, states collect data differently, which accounts for some discrepancies. Sexually abused boys tend to be older than girls and are more likely to be abused by non-family females. Over the past number of years, researchers believe that the occurrences of child sexual abuse have decreased due to more attention to sexual abuse and more consistent means of punishing perpetrators. Children who live in homes with biological parents are less likely to be victims of sexual abuse than children in single-parent or stepfamily homes. Victimization occurs in a variety of settings, including the home, and may occur spontaneously or be planned by the perpetrator for some time. **Grooming the victim,** as will be discussed below, is one of the maneuvers used by perpetrators. The use of force does occur often, which may have detrimental emotional outcomes (Crimes Against Children Research Center, UNH, 2010).

As stated above, child sexual abuse generally is reported long after the fact, with accidental disclosure being the most common form of disclosure for young children. Researchers have found that it is not uncommon for young children who are victims of sexual abuse to wait until adolescence or adulthood to disclose (Copeland, Keeler, Argold, and Costello, 2007). Frequently the disclosure is made accidently or unintentionally by the child confiding in a friend who tells a parent. A classic study by Sorenson and Snow (1991) with a large sample found that there are four basic stages that disclosure takes. First, the child is in denial and denies the abuse to others. Second is disclosure followed by recantation in which the child recants the denial. Lastly, the fourth stage is the reaffirmation of the abuse. Recanting the abuse tends to be based on pressure from an adult. The most effective way for disclosure to happen is for the child, or adult, for that matter, to be asked directly about being abused.

Effects of Child Sexual Abuse

Children who are sexually abused come from chaotic and unstable families. Researchers have to take care with complex analysis to ferret out the effects of sexual abuse from the effects of the chaotic family. The effects of child sexual abuse vary according to a number of variables, including the type of abuse and degree of severity (Putnam, 2003). For example, not all sexual abuse includes being touched. In most cases of child sexual abuse there are negative consequences because the experience lacks consent; it changes the relationship with the perpetrator, who is often a family member or known to the child, and engages the child in activity that is age inappropriate. Children are not developmentally ready for a sexual experience and one that is forced or non-consensual produces negative and even traumatic side effects. Some of the most common effects found from clinical and nonclinical samples include depression and Post-Traumatic Stress Disorder (PTSD).

While children do not ordinarily link sexual abuse with emotional difficulties, studies find that there is a direct correlation. Children who were sexually abused will score higher on depression measures than children who were not sexually abused (Putnam, 2003). They also are more likely to be suicidal, experience greater levels of anxiety, and have lower levels of self-esteem. Depression associated with childhood sexual abuse stems from internalizing the experience, which also leads to a lower sense of self-esteem and self-worth. Children may feel that they somehow are responsible for the abuse, and instead of blaming the perpetrator they turn it inward on themselves, which is sometimes referred to as **survivor's shame**.

Children of sexual abuse who develop depression may also suffer from poor eating habits and not getting enough sleep. Eating disorders, such as **bulimia** and **anorexia**, can develop because of an overemphasis on the body. Body image and concern about appearance may be disguised ways to attempt to control more negative and unacceptable emotions (Thompson and Wonderlich, 2004). Consequently, the emotional disorders may continue throughout the lifespan in the form of eating disorders, sleep deprivation, confusion, disorientation, and anxiety disorders.

Childhood sexual abuse can prevent and hinder the development of normal friendships and relationship with peers. Generally, the impairment of forming and maintaining relationships depend of the severity of the abuse. The longer the abuse occurred and the severity of the abuse is directly related to the degree of emotional dysfunction. The effect on future relationship formation can be very great, especially the reticence of developing intimate relationships (Putnam, 2003).

Childhood sexual abuse can result in a severe anxiety disorder known as PTSD, which is characterized by flashbacks of previously negative experiences that affect present coping and appropriately response to stimuli. This re-experiencing of the events causes muted and sometimes avoided responses to normal experiences. Although PTSD affects both children and adults, symptoms vary according to a number of variables. While PTSD can be caused by a variety of conditions, one that does not have to happen, that does not happen automatically, and can and should be avoided is sexual abuse. Researchers have focused in recent years on the long-term effects of trauma and its relationship to the development of PTSD. There is also concern that traumatic events such as sexual abuse may alter the developmental trajectory of abused children. Although a number of circumstances are related to the development of PTSD in children, none is more egregious than sexual abuse. Most experiences related to PTSD occur from physical harm, which can be reexperienced periodically from stimuli that would be considered innocuous. Although most people develop symptoms of PTSD soon after the traumatic event, some do not present with symptoms until some future date. The sexual abuse of a child is most damaging when it occurs over time, when the perpetrator is part of the family's inner circle, and when it involves physical touching or rape. Some findings suggest that adults who developed PTSD as children from physical and sexual abuse have increased levels of cortisol when reviewing traumatic situations in an experimental setting (Schmahl, Vermetten, Elzinga, and Bremner, 2003).

Neuroscientists have found that child sexual abuse alters genetic patterns, suggesting that it may be possible in the future to identify various mental or emotional disorders through analyzing genetic patterns and formulate treatment modalities according to these patterns (Ressler, Burgess, and Douglas (1988)). There is also evidence that different types of traumatic events may have different effects on gene activity. For example, one recent study compared persons who develop PTSD from abuse with persons who developed PSTSD from other causes, and found differences in the activity of genes. The group that developed PTSD from abuse was more likely to have genes related to the nervous and immune systems affected, while PTSD associated with other causes showed greater alteration in gene death and the rate of growth of genes.

Studies confirm that later effects of sexual abuse affect females more than males. For example, Filipas and Ullman (2006) found that females blame themselves for the abuse and use more coping strategies of denial than do male victims of sexual abuse. In addition, females report more symptoms of PTSD than males, especially when the disclosure of the abuse was delayed. Generally, the researchers also found that disclosing the abuse to others did not elicit negative reactions.

The effects of PTSD caused by sexual abuse of children, as described by Browne and Finkelhor (1986), included four steps. First, the child is traumatically sexualized, meaning that the natural development of sexual behavior has been interrupted and the child may have difficulty with sexual expressions throughout the lifespan. Second, the sexually abused child may feel betrayed by family members, particularly if there appeared to be little effort to protect the children from the abuse. It is not uncommon that girls will feel betrayed by their mothers. Third, the reaction of others to the disclosure or knowledge of the abuse may be negative stereotyping that affects the self-esteem of the child. Fourth, sexually abused children often feel powerless to stop the abuse, and may, in fact, give up resistance since they see no way to prevent or stop it.

PTSD effects have been described in several different models. According to Kerr (2011), **PTSD** reflects either a single traumatic event labeled as **Type I**, or long-term effects referred to as Type II. Type I can reflect single traumatic events that are psychologically damaging although they occur only one time. On the other hand, **Type II PTSD** typically develops from long-term repeated abuse in which the child suffers ego damage.

Intrafamilial Sexual Abuse (Incest)

Most cultures have laws forbidding sexual intercourse between close kin, although there is some variation. In the past, the incest taboo referred to sexual relations between a parent and a child, but now encompasses a broader meaning of sexual relations within the family, including step relationships, referred to as intrafamilial (Glasser and Kolvin, 2001). Four decades ago sexual abuse of a child within the family was considered rare, but based on ongoing and recent research, it is now believed to be a major family and social problem (Denov, 2004).

Female Sexual Perpetrators

The common view that the male is the perpetrator of sexual abuse and the female is the victim obfuscates the reality that some victims are male. Male victimization tends to go unnoticed and female perpetrators tend to be less identified or punished (Denov, 2003). Researchers and clinicians alike pay little attention to females as perpetrators. A few researchers have raised unanswered questions about the process and occurrence of female sexual abuse. Traditional sexual scripts for males and females in which males are viewed as aggressors and females as passive in sexual relations further reduce efforts to focus on female abuse. Women are viewed in all societies as being less aggressive, emotionally supportive of others, and having greater caretaking skills. Not only does the cultural script minimize females as sexually aggressive but it also casts doubt that abuse perpetrated by women is as harmful as abuse perpetrated by men. The literature on female perpetrators comes mainly from analyzing case material and self-report studies. This analysis found a higher likelihood of perpetration of child sexual abuse for females than case material. This difference in case material and self-reports may emanate partly from the influence of cultural sexual scripts in the court system, which tends to ignore cases involving women as perpetrators. Sexual abuse by women is viewed as being less reported by victims than sexual abuse by males. Researchers have also found that abuse by females is less reported by both male and female victims. Overall, fewer cases are prosecuted by the court systems, and when a case is prosecuted, females are given considerably lower sentences.

Gender biases in sexual abuse cases were found in a study conducted by Hetherton and Beardsall (1999, as cited in Denov, 2004). The research consisted of two groups of professionals, social workers and law enforcement personnel, who were given the same case scenario with males and females as the perpetrators. Both groups were consistent in concluding that female abuse was less severe and needed less intervention than the male abuse. No doubt this pervasive gender bias attitude contributes to fewer cases reported and prosecuted.

Mandatory Reporting of Abuse

Professionals who work with children are required to report suspected child abuse and neglect. The professionals in the majority of states and provinces include medical personnel, school personnel, therapists, social workers, child care workers, and law enforcement personnel (Child Welfare Information Gateway, 2012). Since **mandatory reporting of sexual abuse** is governed by state law, some states require additional persons than those mentioned above. For example, in California mandatory reporting is required for personnel in businesses or groups that provide activities for children, such as camps or recreational facilities. In approximately 18 states and Puerto Rico, in addition to professionals working with children, all persons are required to be mandatory reporters. All states allow anyone to report suspected abuse. Most states suspend **privileged communication**, communication between a professional and a client that is confidential, in the case of abuse. The attorney-client confidential communication is most often allowed by states. Generally, the disclosure of the name of the person reporting abuse is kept confidential in most states, but some have special provisions for the release of the name.

Perpetrators

Much as been written and hypothesized about perpetrators, with disparate points of view and on-going discussion. It is clear from the preponderance of research literature that most child sexual perpetrators are not pedophiles and do not have a sexual preference for young, prepubescent children. Instead, child sexual perpetrators tend to have the capacity for sexual abuse of children in addition to other sexual deviant behavior, such as rape of adult females. What this means is that sexual exploitation of children, except for a small minority of abusers who prefer young children as sexual objects, represents a wider and more pervasive problems in society.

One of the questions that is commonly asked is: Does a link exist between being abused as a child and committing acts of abuse as an adult, or the **victim-to-perpetrator paradigm?** A substantial body of literature has addressed the victim-to-perpetrator paradigm to understand the overall phenomenon of sexual abuse and victimization. While large in scope, there still exists debate over the meanings of the findings that link victimization and perpetrators (Glasser and Kolvin, 2001). For example, there are more girls victimized than boys, but few female perpetrators. Some studies, however, conclude that the number of male victims may be much larger than reported because most experts believe that males tend to underreport sexual abuse. Most studies find that approximately 30% of perpetrators were victims of sexual assault as children, while only 11% of non-abusers were abused. Researchers also find that children who are victims of sexual abuse tend to be raised in chaotic and dysfunctional homes, which may contaminate a direct link to the victim-perpetrator model. Generally speaking, however, the victim-perpetrator link tends to be supported for males, but not for females.

Sexual Abuse and Recidivism Rates

Sexual offender recidivism rates, the rate at which offenders commit other sexual crimes after prosecution, range between 10 and 15%, although some abusers have higher rates (Harris et, al., 2003). Researchers have identified two types of sexual offenders, those engaging in deviant sexual activities and those with antisocial personality disorder; the latter of which commit the most heinous sexual crimes. Contributing factors for persons who commit sexual crimes are deviant sexual behavior, hostile and unstable family background, inability to form appropriate long-term affectionate bonds, and accepting attitudes toward sexual aggression.

Sexual Predator Laws

Although the majority of sexual abuse cases are committed by someone known to the victim, much effort on the part of the state and federal governments has been made to curb stranger sexual abuse, which tends to be more heinous and usually involves abduction, rape and murder. Child abductions receive much media attention and outcry from parent advocacy groups. Federal legislation, both to prevent future sexual abuse and to punish offenders, has been enacted on the federal level over the past 20 years.

One of the most well-known laws is referred to as **Megan's Law**, which allows for registration of sex offenders and community notification of their residences (Megan's Law: Sex Offenders Registration and Exclusion Law, 2001). The federal law was entitled the Jacob Wetterling Sexual Abuse Act of 1994. Megan's Law, which resulted after Megan Kanka was lured from her home by a neighbor who had previously been convicted of sex crimes, has been bolstered by other legislation to make it a stronger deterrent for perpetrators. This legislation includes the Adam Walsh Child Protection and Safety

Act of 2006 (para 1), which enlarged reporting jurisdictions, including Native American citizens, and increased the number of sexual crimes for registration. The purpose of this is act is to follow discharged sexual offenders after they have served time. The registry, consisting of online state websites, includes the offender's name, place of residence and sexual offenses. Failure to comply with the law, which includes updates of present status, is a federal crime.

Jessica's Law was passed in Florida and subsequently in several other states after the abduction and murder of Jessica Lundsford by a known sexual offender who lived next door. This law made lewd acts against a child under the age of 12 a life felony, established mandatory prison sentences of 25 years, lifetime electronic monitoring, and lifetime probation after serving time (Jessica's Law Now, 2014).

The question often arises regarding the effectiveness and constitutionality of sexual offender laws. Recidivism rates for persons convicted of sex offenses, which are generally lower than the general population, range from 15–20% depending on a number of factors, including the type of offense and the treatment offered. Prison sentences without treatment have not been found to be effective in reducing recidivism (Aos, Miller, Drake, 2006). Repeat offenders, especially male pedophiles, are the most likely to commit additional crimes. Not only are recidivism rates high for offenders who target strangers but they commit the most heinous sex crimes. Most experts believe that early detection and treatment are the most effective in reducing sexual crimes and decreasing recidivism rates (Worling, Litteljohn, and Bookalam, 2010). Studies have found that prison time does not reduce the risk of committing future sexual crimes, while cognitive-behavioral treatment does reduce the risk (Aos, Miller, and Drake, 2006).

Researchers have begun to compile data on sexual offenses to determine what factors are effective in reducing the occurrence of such crimes and the recidivism rates. Recent research by Prescott and Rockoff (2008) found some interesting and incongruous findings. For example, while community notification may deter some persons from committing sexual crimes, they seem to increase the recidivism rate of those who commit crimes. The researchers hypothesized, without empirical evidence, that because of their "status" as sex offenders they tend to be unemployed, live in poor and unsafe housing, and lack a supportive social network. In other words, sex offenders are already at the bottom on the social ladder and, therefore, there would be few additional costs to continuing sexual exploitation of others. They further hypothesized that life in prison may be more rewarding than life in a rejecting society.

Prescott and Rockoff (2008) are not alone in their concerns about the full effect of sex offender laws on rates of sex crimes and related crimes. According to Lancester (2011), sex offender laws fail to accomplish their purposes of reducing the occurrence of sex crimes and providing appropriate treatment for offenders. One of the main reasons for this failure, according to Lancester, is the unwieldy size of the state and federal registries, which now exceed 700,000 names. Because the federal registry is a joining of the state registries and is governed by state laws, there are differences in the types of offenses that make up the registries across states. In some states, a person's name

TABLE 5.3 History of laws and sexual abuse

- Jacob Wetterling Crimes Against Children Sexually Violent Offender Registration Act—1994
- The Pam Lychner Sexual Offender Tracking and Identification Registration Act—1996
- Megan's Law—1996
- Jacob Wetterling Improvements Act—1997
- Perfection of Children From Sexual Predators Act—1998
- The Campus Sexual Protection Act—2000
- Prosecutorial Remedies and Other Tools to End the Exploitation of Children Today (PROTECT) Act—2003
- Adam Walsh Child Protection and Safety Act—2006
- Department of Justice, Office of the Attorney General, Applicability of the Ex-Offender Registration and Notification Act
- Keeping Internet Devoid of Predators (KIDS) Act
- Kids of 2008

appears on the registry for urinating in public, for minors engaging in consensual sex or sexting, and for sexual explicit messaging with peers through social media such as Facebook. Others states include only persons who have engaged in forcible rape or other acts of sexual exploitation or violence. This inconsistency raises the question of the arbitrariness of sex offender laws and whether some persons are inappropriately identified as sex offenders. In addition, **mandatory sentencing** and **civil commitment laws** in some states have provisions that offenders deemed inappropriate for release after the original sentence has been served may be retained indefinitely, or if released, must have an electronic monitor for life. Further, some states such as California prohibit sex offenders from public access to areas frequented by children and restrict their places of residence.

Opponents to the extensive sexual offender laws believe that they are unfair and excessive punishment and violate basic human rights (Lancester, 2011). They advocate for repealing the most restrictive laws beginning with public restrictions. In addition, opponent advocates recommend that registries be open to law enforcement officials, but not to the general public. According to Lancester, public registries marginalize offenders and encourage recidivism, believing that offenders have little to lose by continued offenses. In addition, they believe that the evidence supporting such restrictions is not verified by research data. The "one size fits all" approach to sexual offenders belies the fact that offenders are not a homogenous group. Advocates for strict laws point out that while registry laws may not reduce the occurrence of sex crimes, they have been effective in making arrests after crimes have been committed.

False Allegations

Not all allegations of sexual abuse are true and some researchers have noted a range of approximately 5% false reports in recent years. One reason for the number of false reports may be due to the increase in mandatory reporting and greater attention to sexual educational settings. However, since many abused children do retract their accusations, the actual number of false reports is hard to determine. Gardner (1989) hypothesized that the **parental alienation syndrome,** in which one parent demonizes the other parent, most likely the father, to the child during times of conflict between the parents, such as in custody battles, only further confuses and obviates the situation.

Another ongoing issue is the actual investigation of the accusation. For example, one of the most flagrant problems is when the investigator conducting the interview with the child asks leading questions. Unless investigators are specifically trained to interview children, their own biases may prevent an open and realistic conclusion. The use of anatomical dolls can also produce false reporting and requires considerable training not to bias the child's responses. The court proceeding may cause a child to relive the abusive situation; videotape or transcripts of the child's statements could protect the child from further damage. Court proceedings tend to be protracted and the child may be on the stand a number of times, including during cross-examination. The effect on the child who testifies in court is also heavily influenced by whether the case has a positive outcome or negative outcome. If the perpetrator is found guilty, the outcome for the child tends to be positive.

Treatment of Sexual Abuse

Initially one of the most important functions for CPS is to remove the child from the situation in which abuse is occurring (Filipas and Ullman, 2006). A decision is made by CPS as to whether the child can remain in the family. Frequently, removing the child may be required if the abuser is a family member who lives at the same address as the child. If the offender is a parent, detailed information about that parent, including past history of abuse, is necessary to determine future plans. The non-abusing parent must also be evaluated to determine the extent of his/her knowledge of the abuse and whether the parent failed to protect the child. If either the offender or the child is removed from the home, visitation becomes an important issue to determine. Investigators must also decide if the offender has potential to be rehabilitated.

The abused child has reduced ability to trust others, especially when the abuser was a close trusted family member. The inability to trust is further eroded when the non-abusing parent withholds support and fails to fully believe the child's accusations. When a non-family member is the abuser, the child may still feel betrayed by parents not protecting him/her from this acquaintance (Filipas and Ullman, 2006). The abused child will feel a multiplicity of emotions, including blaming him- or herself, self-identity problems, and fear and anxiety. In response to these emotions, the child may react in a number of ways that can result in various therapeutic interventions. Some children may publicly act out sexually, such as masturbating frequently. Curtailing this inappropriate public behavior and dealing with the over-sexualized behavior is essential for reducing the likelihood of the child being a sexual perpetrator in the future.

Other treatment issues revolve around the relationship between the mother and the victim. The mother-victim relationship is the key to family reunification. If this relationship lacks support, or if the abuse caused a relationship distancing to occur, repair is needed before reunification can commence. The risk of future re-victimization is reduced when the mother-victim relationship is cohesive. Generally speaking, the mother-victim relationship refers more to the mother-daughter dyad than to the mother-son dyad.

Key Terms

Child abuse and neglect

Battered child syndrome

Physical abuse

Spanking (corporal punishment)

Depression

Anxiety disorder

Mood disorder

Conditional spanking

Pruning

Myelination

Mandatory reporting of sex abuse

Privileged communication

Victims to perpetrator paradigm

Sexual offender recidivism rates

Hypothalamic-pituitary-adrenal (HPA) axis

Sympathetic nervous system

Serotonin

Post-Traumatic Stress Disorder (PTSD)

Subdural and retina hemorrhage

Neglected children

Dual-career

Domestic violence

Prenatal environment

Failure to thrive

Megan's Law

Jessica's Law

Mandatory sentencing

Civil commitment laws

Failure to protect

Chronic stress

Child sexual abuse

Grooming the victim

Survivor's shame

Bulimia

Anorexia

Type I PTSD

Type II PTSD

Interfamilial abuse

Parental alienation syndrome

Mother-victim relationship

1. Discuss the four basic stages of sexual abuse.

2. Have cases of child abuse and neglect declined in recent years? Explain your answer.

3. Discuss the link between physical punishment and abuse. Should measures be taken to curtail spanking as a form of discipline of children?

4. Why is neglect of children less likely to be prosecuted? Should more effort go into reducing the occurrence of neglect?

5. Discuss child sexual abuse. Are prevention and treatment efforts on the right track?

6. Discuss effects of child sexual abuse. How does sexual abuse affect the brain?

7. Discuss the difference in female and male sexual victimization. Should more effort be placed on reducing acts committed by female perpetrators?

8. Do the drawbacks of mandatory reporting of sex acts outweigh the positive effects? Explain your answer.

9. Are sexual predator laws helpful, or do they do more harm than good, given that sexual predators do not commit the bulk of cases?

10. What are false allegations in sexual cases? What efforts should be made to reduce the occurrence of false allegations?

Debate Activity for Students

Consider the following proposition: Treatment for sexual perpetrators, such as in Coalinga State Hospital, is a waste of taxpayer's money.

- Review refereed literature on this topic.
- Develop three arguments for the proposition.
- Develop three arguments against the proposition.
- How do the arguments relate to other systems, such as the community or culture?
- Is there common ground?
- What are the long-term consequences?
- What common-ground solutions should be offered?

REFERENCES

Adam Walsh Child Protection and Safety Act. (2006). The National Conference of State Legislatures. Retrieved March 9, 2014 from http://www.ncsl.org/research/civil-and-criminal-justice/adam-walshchild-protection-and-safety-act.aspx.

Afifi, T. O., Mota, N. P., Dasiewiez, P., MacMillan, H. L., & Sareen, J. (2012). Physical punishment and mental disorders: Results from a nationally represented U.S. sample. *Pediatrics*, 130(2), 184–192.

Aos, S., Miller, M., & Drake, E. (2006). Evidence-based adult corrections programs: What works and what does not. Olympia: Washington State Institute for Public Policy.

Bragg, H. L. (2003). *Child protection in families experiencing domestic violence.* U.S. Department of Health and Human Services, Administration for Children and Families, Administration on Children, Youth and Families, Children's Bureau, Office of Child Abuse and Neglect, Washington, DC.

Belsky, J. (1996). Parent, infant, and social-contextual antecedents of father-son attachment security. *Developmental Psychology*, 5, 905–913.

Belsky, J. (1986). Infant day care: A cause for concern? *Zero to Three*, 6(4), 1–7.

Broman-Fulks, J., Ruggiero, K. J., Hanson, R. F., Smith, D. W., Resnick, H. S., Kilpatrick, D. G., & Saunders, B. S. (2007). Sexual assault disclosed in relation to adolescent mental health: Results from the national survey of adolescents. *Journal of Clinical Child and Adolescent and Psychology*, 36(2), 260–266.

Browne, A., & Finkelhor, D. (1986). Initial and long-term effects: A review of the research. In D. Finkelhor (Ed.), *A sourcebook on child sexual abuse* (pp. 143–179). Beverly Hills, CA: Sage.

Child Abuse Prevention and Treatment Act (CAPTA) Reauthorization Act of 2010 (P.L. 111–320), § 3.

Centers for Disease Control and Prevention. (2014). Together for girls: Scope of the problem—sexual violence against girls. Retrieved March 8, 2014 from http://www.cdc.gov/violencePrevention/sexualviolence/together/index.html.

Child Welfare Information Gateway. (2012). *Mandatory reporters of child abuse and neglect.* Washington, DC: U.S. Department of Health and Human Services.

Corcoran, J., & Nichols-Casebolt, A. (2004). Risk and Resilience: Ecological framework for assessment and goal formulation. *Child and Adolescent Social Work Journal*, 21(3), 211–218.

Copeland, W. D., Keeler, G., Angold, A., & Costello, E. J. (2007). Traumatic events and post-traumatic stress in childhood. *Archives of General Psychiatry*, 64, 577–584.

Crimes against Child Research Center, UNH (2010). *Trends in children's exposure to violence, 2003–2011*. Retrieved March 15, 2014 from www.unh.edu/ccrc//.

Ernst, J., Meyer, M., & DePanfiflis, D. (2004). Housing characteristics and adequacy of the physical care of children: An exploratory analysis. *Child Welfare*, 85(5), 437–452.

Denov, M. S. (2004). The long-term effects of child sexual abuse by female perpetrators: A qualitative study of male and female victims. *Journal of Interpersonal Violence*, 19, 1137–1156.

Fang, X., Brown, D. S., Florence, C. S., & Mercy, J. A. (2012). The economic burden of child maltreatment in the United States and implications for treatment. *Child Abuse and Neglect*, 36(2), 156–165.

Filipas, H. H., & Ullman, S. E. (2006). Child sexual abuse, coping response, self-blame, post-traumatic stress disorder, and adult sexual revitalization. *Journal of Interpersonal Violence*, 21(5) 552–572.

Finkelhor, D., & Jones, L. M. (2004). *Sexual abuse in the 1990s: Evidence for possible causes. Juvenile Justice Bulletin*. U.S. Department of Justice, Office of Justice Programs, Office of Juvenile Justice and Delinquency Prevention.

Fries, A. B., & Pollak, S. D. (2004). Emotion, understanding, in post-institutionalized Eastern European children. *Developmental Psychopathology*, 16(2), 355–369.

Gardner, R. (1989). Differentiating between bona fide and fabricated allegations of sexual abuse of children. *Journal of the American Academy of Matrimonial Lawyers*, 5, 1–25.

Gaudin, J. (1993). *Child neglect: A guide to intervention*. National Center for Child Abuse and Neglect, U.S. Department of Health and Human Services, Administration for Children and Families.

Glasser, M., & Kolvin, I. (2001). Cycle of child sexual abuse: Links between being a victim and becoming a perpetrator. *The British Journal of Psychiatry*, 179(6), 882–894.

Goldman, J., Salus, M. K., Wolcott, D., & Kennedy, K. Y. (2003). *A coordinated response to child abuse and neglect: The foundation for practice*. Office of Child Abuse and Neglect, Children's Bureau.

Greder, K., & Brotherson, M. J. (2001). Stress and coping: Low-income mothers feeding their children. *National Council on Family Relations*, 42(2), F5–F8.

Giovannoni, J. M.,& Becerra, R. M. (1979). *Defining child abuse*. New York: The Free Press.

Harris, G. T., Rice, M. E., Quinsey, V .L., Lalumiere M. L., Doer, D., & Lang, C. (2003). *A multisite comparison of actuarial risk instruments for sex offenders*. Center for Addiction and Mental Health University of Toronto, Correctional Services of Canada.

Hildyard, K. L., & Wolfe, D. A. (2002). Child neglect: Developmental issues and outcomes. *Child Abuse & Neglect*, 26, 679–695.

Jessica's Law Now. (2014). Retrieved March 9, 2014, from http://jessicaslawnow.wordpress.com/about-jessicas-law/.

Kantor, G. K., & Little, L. (2003). Defining the boundaries of child neglect: When does domestic violence equate with parental failure to protect? *Journal of Interpersonal Violence*, 18, 138–155.

Kelley, S. J. (2002). Child maltreatment in the context of substance abuse. In J. E. B. Myers, L. Berliner, J. Briere, C. T. Hendrix, C. Jenny, and T.A Reid (Eds.). *The APSAC Handbook on Child Maltreatment* (2nd ed.). (pp. 105–117). Thousand Oaks: Sage.

Kerr, L. (2011). Dissociation in late modern American society: Defense against soul? ProQuest.

Lancester, R. N. (2011). *Sex panic and the punitive state*. Berkeley, CA: University of California Press.

Larzelere, R. E., & Kuhn, B. R. (2005). Comparing child outcomes of physical punishment and alternative disciplinary tactics: a meta-analysis. *Clinical Child and Family Psychology Review*, 8(1), 1–37.

Megan's Law: Sex Offenders Registration and Exclusion Law. (2001). Office of the Attorney General, State of California, Department of Justice.

Myers, J. E. B. (2008). A short history of child protection in America. *Family Law Quarterly*, 42(3), 449–463.

Navalta, C. P., Polcari, A., Webster, D. M., Boghossian, A., & Teicher, M. H. (2006). Effects of childhood sexual abuse on neuropsychological and cognitive function in college women. *Journal of Neuropsychiatry and Clinical Neuroscience*, 18(1), 45–53.

Needell, B., Webster, D., Armijo, M. et al. (2012). Child Welfare Services Report for California. Retrieved March 8, 2014 from http://cssr.berkeley.edy/ucb_childwelfare.

Ochsner, K. N., & Gross, J. J. (2005). Review of the cognitive control of emotion. *Trends in Cognitive Science*, 9(5), 242–249.

Panel on Research on Child Abuse and Neglect (1993). Commission on Behavioral and Social Sciences and Education, National Research Council. Understanding Child Abuse and Neglect. Washington, DC: National Academy Press; 1993:208.

Pollak, S. D., Nelson, C. A., Schlaak, M. F., Roeber, B. J., Wewerka, S. S., Wiik, K. L., Frenn, K. A., Loman, M. M., & Gunner, M. R. (2010). Neurodevelopmental effects of early deprivation in post-institutionalized children. *Child Development*, 81(1), 224–236.

Prescott, J. J., & Rockoff, J. E. (2008). Do Sex Offender Registration and Notification Laws Affect Criminal Behavior? Retrieved March 9, 2014, from http://ssrn.com/abstract=110066.

Putnam, F. W. (2003). Ten-year update review: Child sexual abuse. *Journal of the American Academy of Child and Adolescent Psychiatry*, 42(3), 269–278.

Radford, L., & Hester, M. (2006). Mothering through domestic violence. *British Journal of Social Work*, 37(4), 770–772.

Reece, R. M., & Sege, R. (2000). Childhood head injuries: Accidental or inflicted? *Archives of Pediatric and Adolescent Medicine*, 154, 11–15.

Ressler, R. K., Burgess, A. W., & Douglas, J. E. (1988). *Sexual homicide: Patterns and motives*. Lexington, MA: Lexington Books.

Samuelson, K. W., Krueger, C. E., Burnett, C., & Wilson, C. K. (2010). Neuropsychological functioning in children with post-traumatic stress disorder. *Child Neuropsychology*, 16(2), 119–133.

Schmahl, C.G., Vermetten, E., Elzinga, B.M., & Douglas-Bremner, J. (2003). Magnetic resonance of hippocampal and amygdala volume in women with childhood abuse and borderline personality disorder. *Psychiatry Research*, 122(3), 193–198.

Schnizer, P., & Ewigman, B. (2005). Child deaths resulting from inflicted injuries: Household risk factors and perpetrator characteristics, *Pediatrics*, 116, 687–693.

Sorensen, T., & Snow, B. (1991). How children tell: The process of disclosure of child sexual abuse. *Child Welfare*, 70, 3–15.

Sowell, E. R., Peterson, B. S., Thompson, P. M., Welcome, S. E., Henkenius, A. L., & Toga, A. W. (2003). Mapping cortical change across the human life span. *Nature Neuroscience*, 6(3), 309–315.

Springer, K. W., Sheridan, J., Kuo, D., & Carnes, M. (2007). Long-term physical and mental health consequences of childhood physical abuse: Results from a large population-based sample of men and women. *Child Abuse and Neglect*, 31(5), 517–530.

Straus, M. A. (2000). Corporal punishment and primary prevention of physical abuse. *Child Abuse and Neglect*, 24(9), 1109–1114.

Stowman, S.A., & Donahue, B. (2005). Assessing child neglect: A review of standardized measures. *Aggressive and Violent Behavior*, 10, 491–512.

Thomlison, B. (2004). Child Maltreatment: A risk and protection factor perspective. In M. W. Fraser (Ed.), *Risk and resilience in childhood: An ecological perspective* (2nd ed.) (pp. 89–131). Washington, DC: National Association of Social Workers Press (NASW).

Thompson, K. M., & Wonderlich, S. A. (2004). Child sexual abuse and eating disorders. In J. K. Thompson (Ed.), *Handbook of eating disorders and obesity* (pp. 679–694). Hoboken, NJ: Wiley & Sons.

Tolan, P. H., Sherrod, L. R., Gorman-Smith, D., & Henry, D. B. (2004). Building protection, support, and opportunity for inner-city children and youth and their families. In K. I. Maton, C. J. Schellenbach, B. J. Leadbeater, and A. L. Solarz (Eds.), *Investing in youth, families and communities: Strengths-based research and policy* (pp. 193–211). Washington, DC: American Psychological Association.

U.S. Department of Health and Human Services, Administration for Children and Families, Administration on Children, Youth and Families, Children's Bureau. (2011). *Child Maltreatment 2010*. Retrieved August 12, 2013 from http://www.acf.hhs.gov/programs/cb/stats_research/index.htm#can.

Wagner, G. N. (1986). Bitemark identification in child abuse cases. *Pediatric Dentistry*, 8, 96–100.

Walton, A. G. (2012) The long-term effects of spanking. *The Atlantic*, February 24, 2012. Retrieved August 12, 2013 from http://cdn.theatlantic.com/static/mt/assets/food/main%20thumb%20shutter-stock_75783793.jpg.

Watts-English, T., Fortson, B. L., Gibler, N., Hooper, S. R., & DeBellis, M. D. (2006). The psychology of maltreatment in childhood. *Journal of Social Issues*, 62, 717–736.

Wilson, D., & Horner, W. (2005). Chronic child neglect: Needed developments in theory and practice. *Families in Society: The Journal of Contemporary Social Services*, 86(4), 471–481.

Worling, J. R., Litteljohn, A., & Bookalam, M. A. (2010). Twenty-year prospective follow-up study of specialized treatment for adolescents. *Behavior, Science and Law*, 28, 46–57.

Chapter 6

Marjorie's Story

Marjorie McKinnon

I'm going to begin this [chapter] with a story. Mine. Hopefully, everyone reading will identify with parts of it and realize they're in the right place. We all have stories that are different. We all have stories that are the same. Repercussions in the life of an incest victim ripple like waves in a body of water, ones that eventually turn into riptides, undercurrents, and sometimes tidal waves.

My story is a classic example.

In July of 1988, I walked into the office of therapist Marci Taylor, a specialist in the field of childhood sexual abuse. The damage done by my incest had accelerated to the point of despair. It was six months before my third marriage and I had a long history of relationships with alcoholics and abusers, two of them former husbands. Suicidal since my early teens, I had been hospitalized for two nervous breakdowns in my twenties, one the result of a failed suicide attempt. I had hidden my pain behind too much alcohol, promiscuity, compulsive behavior, obsessive relationships and extremes of emotional highs and lows. Only medication, intermittently taken, had kept me functioning for almost twenty-five years.

Two years earlier, I had been engaged to my daughter's father-in-law. Chuck was the first healthy male in my life, a man whose primary aim was making me happy. He became convinced that something traumatizing had happened in my childhood that I didn't remember. His comment, "How could someone as wonderful as you wind up with so many abusive men," not only went right over my head, but irritated me as he began a personal crusade to find out what had happened. I retaliated with anger, tried to end the engagement, and when he refused, began an affair outside the relationship. His response was, "I'll never leave you except through death." Within months, he was diagnosed with lung cancer. Filled with shame and fear for Chuck, I ended the affair and took care of him while he was ill. Even then, a few days before he died, still unable to control my own sexual addiction, I slept not only with another man, but a married one. After Chuck's death, my guilt and shame at what I had done caused despair so great I wished only that I had never failed in my many suicide attempts.

Within a few weeks, I was living with the man who would ultimately set off a trail of such severe abuse that I had to choose between death and entering recovery. I had hit bottom. Having read my private journals without permission, he used my descriptions of previous lovers and infidelities as a whip to taunt me, especially the night I had spent in bed with a married man while Chuck lay dying. Like Pavlov's dog, every time he rang the bell by shaming me about my past, I obeyed whatever his current demand was, for I learned quickly that giving in caused the torment to cease. Subject to his whims, I lived like a prisoner, crippled by his several-times-a-day sexual addiction— which quickly turned into brutal rapes—his need to control what I wore, whom I spoke with, what I said, and even whether I laughed or not.

Within months, my beautiful home looked like a battleground, with bathroom doors he had split in half when I cowered behind them hiding from his rages and sexual obsessions, broken furniture and holes in walls, all evidence of my out-of-control emotions from the terror of his rapes. Once he forced me into making sex videotapes by taunting me about previous infidelities. In the process, I lost my mind as I lay in a fetal position on the floor, calling for my mother. Before we'd been together a year, his need for frequent middle-of-the-night sex was causing painful and confusing flashbacks.

One time, years earlier, in the office of a therapist, I had spied a cartoon. It was of a woman standing in a cage with her hands clenched on the bars, looking outward with terror. The cage had only three sides. That cartoon was so painful that I averted my eyes every time I saw it. It haunted me for years, and became one of the spurs to my entering recovery, for now I could see that I was that woman.

My self-image was so poor that once, in a department store, I saw a woman on the other side of the room and thought desperately, *I would give anything if only I looked like her*. As I walked closer, I realized that her body movements matched mine. I'd been staring in a mirror! Even then, I waved my arms and made faces, then finally touched the glass before I became convinced it was me. You'd think it would have caused me to look at myself in a different light. It didn't. I wasn't ready to believe that there was anything beautiful about me. Even my frequent quip over the years, "If you took sex out of my life, I'd be a near-perfect person," did not encourage me to see that although I had a dark side, there were many gems beneath my surface.

Despite the use of various therapists over the years who had probed my life, none had ever identified incest as the culprit. In my early thirties, my father had admitted to his wrongdoing, making the comment, "It really wasn't so bad, kiddo, they do it in the Appalachian district all the time." Shortly before he died, he again brought it up, then abruptly dropped it. Both times, I buried the reality, the pain too monumental to consider. I was not even sure what the word "incest" meant, and other than a nightmare I'd had when I was younger, one where a steamroller was suffocating me as I lay in my bottom bunk, I had no memory of such things happening. I had relived the "nightmare" hundreds of times throughout my life, on each occasion waking up screaming as I felt the paralyzing terror of being overpowered by an unknown force. The nightmares didn't cease until after my father's death in 1985.

Now, shaking with continuous tremors, I turned once more to therapy. This time it was at the insistence of my family doctor, who had been convinced for many years that incest was the source of my problems.

Marci began my treatment with several sessions of discussions concerning my child-hood. I gave her the same story I had given the others. I was the oldest daughter in a Midwestern Catholic family. My father had delivered me in the middle of a blizzard in northern Minnesota. As the years went by, his interest in me became obsessive. My mother, worn down from having four children in as many years, turned her fifth child, a daughter, over to me to raise. At the age of eight, I had become the family housekeeper and, at the age of nine, a mother. When I was thirteen, I had the "nightmare" that was to haunt me for so many years.

For reasons I didn't understand at the time, during this period our family life changed dramatically. Mom and Dad discarded any semblance of love and togetherness. My sib-lings and I became like mutilated soldiers in the midst of a war, as we wandered through our days in a continual state of anxiety and terror of Dad. He began a crusade to prove me no good, referring to me as "unclean." Most of the time, Mom lay in bed sobbing or in an alcoholic-like stupor where she had me shave her legs, bathe her, and care for her as if she were in the midst of a debilitating illness. I spiraled into despair, becoming not only manic depressive, but suicidal.

I had come from a long line of patriarchal families with fathers who had a strong sense of their own importance and mothers who subjugated their needs to those of the head of the family. We walked on eggs if Dad was in the house, lest we offend him in some way. His word was not only law, but any opinions contrary to his were punishable. This way of life duplicated my father's growing-up years as well as my mother's. It felt normal to me. My mother's motto was: *Even when your father is wrong, he's right.* A few years later, she developed breast cancer, and Dad convinced her that all doctors were quacks, depriving her of the medical care that might have saved her life. She died angry, resentful, and confused about her own value system.

At the age of eighteen, after a beating from my father that almost killed me, I stuffed a few belongings into a pillowcase and ran. Once on my own, I entered what was to become more than thirty years of unhealthy choices and abusive relationships.

After hearing the story of my life and descriptions of my current victimization, Marci gave me an assignment. I was to draw pictures at various intervals of my life with my left hand, depicting emotions in different colors. I found the exercise rather silly until I sat at the kitchen table and began drawing. There, memories I had forgotten surfaced. When I got to the age of thirteen, I drew a picture of a young girl lying on a bottom bunk bed. A gray-haired man stood in the doorway. I grabbed a red crayon and wrote: *Help me! Help me!* across the face of it, before bursting into tears.

Within days, I entered a twelve-step program, and through hypnosis and more therapy sessions with Marci, began to see the truth, not only of what had happened to me, but the impact it had on my life and the kinds of decisions I had made. At the age of thirteen, I had become my father's unwilling mistress. Eventually, my mother discovered Dad's middle-of-the-night rapes while I slept with a rosary clutched in my hand. Unable to deal with the thought that her husband was the perpetrator of such a crime, she made me the scapegoat, frequently taunting my father into beating me with a belt. Even those memories were never defined in my head as child abuse, only as strict parenting.

Recovery, prolonged by my decision to stay with my abuser, lasted for almost five years. It was like trying to swim upstream with heavy chains hanging around my neck. I worked a rigorous and honest twelve-step program, attended seminars on child abuse and self-esteem, read recovery books, listened to recovery CDs, chronicled my life story, journalized on a regular basis, constructed a "Magic Mirror" (you will find out more about this later), and traveled out of state to meet my father's relatives, then pieced together the family history that had set me up for self-destruction. In short, I did all the things that I later utilized in developing REPAIR.

As I traveled across what I had begun calling the Bridge of Recovery, tools were periodically placed in my path, not only to see the truth, but to empower me. Later on in the program, I will more fully describe this bridge. I recall the day my daughter gave me a workbook entitled *I Never Knew I Had a Choice*. The title alone set off gratifying leaps in behavior changes. Another time, while shopping at a swap meet, I found a sweatshirt that proclaimed, "What part of NO don't you understand?" Whenever I wore it, I felt stronger. A brochure in a pharmacist's office stated, "Losing your freedom of choice is a bitter pill to swallow." It caused me to sob for days until I finally tapped into a new truth. It was all the start, at first in baby steps, not only to saying no when an unhealthy choice was offered, but realizing that I could make my own healthy choices.

In the middle of my recovery, my youngest daughter inadvertently commented on what had happened sexually to her sisters when they were little. I froze with terror, and within minutes, after calling my two older daughters, discovered that they too had been "incested" by my second husband while we were married. Grief strangled me as my need to become totally healthy accelerated in the hope that it would change the lives of my children. As I thought of my grandchildren and their children, a sense of urgency overwhelmed me. It was only later that I found out that children of an untreated incest victim stand a five times greater chance of being incested themselves, because incest is a multi-generational illness. This knowledge compounded my guilt.

My eldest daughter, alcoholic and bulimic, had already duplicated my penchant for going from man to man. One of her sisters had spent ten years in a nightmare marriage to a violent and unstable man. To add to the burden was my despair that I may have contributed in some way to my youngest daughter, at seventeen, being raped at gunpoint by a masked bandit. She, too, was currently married to a man who was so abusive that one time he pointed a gun to her head and forced her to relive her rape.

I staggered at the realization that four out of five of my family members were victims of sexual abuse. To make the statistics more ironic, my son was an officer on the Los Angeles Police Department (LAPD). He had never been sexually abused and was happily married, stable, and disciplined. He not only made healthy choices on a regular basis, but it was difficult for him to understand why others didn't. On the day he graduated from the LAPD, he had hugged me and said, "I think I can make a difference, Mom." His words placed a balance in the midst of my torment. I could only hope that his career choice would one day save others from perpetrators.

In October of 1992, I journeyed back to the small town where I had been molested and raped by my father. There, armed with the courage of four and a half years of recovery, I confronted the ghosts from my past by going into my former bedroom. Although it was the hardest thing I have ever done, it empowered me. I came home, forced my abuser out of the house, got a restraining order against him, filed for a divorce, and spent the next six months doing post-recovery work.

Today, I can hardly remember what it feels like to be suicidal. Periodically, and with a certain wry humor, I ask my Higher Power to "please disregard previous instructions." Today, I make healthy choices and am filled with a sense of wonder and enchantment. I am strong, centered, stable, joyful, disciplined, and self-sufficient. My shame is a thing of the past, and despair and hopelessness are no longer a part of my life. I still experience sad times and stress, but now I have the right tools to handle any problems that arise. Today, the motto above my desk reads: *If I had known life was going to turn out this good, I would have started it earlier.*

No matter how painful your past, how filled with shame your life has been, it is never too late to change. Fifty years ago, "incest" was a word few people knew. Those who did thought it was biblical in origin and certainly had nothing to do with what Dad or Grandpa or Uncle Willy was doing to us in the middle of the night. Today, so much help is available that no one needs to suffer. All it takes is the right program and the commitment to follow it. It won't be easy. Most things of value have a price. But the price is small compared to the waiting reward. The journey itself, arduous though it may be, will awaken your frightened inner child. It will teach her (or him) emotionally healthy behavior and validate lost treasures, those parts of ourselves we've been unable to see.

When I was in recovery, I heard a lot about the "inner child." It was not an unknown expression. In 1963, Dr. W. Hugh Missildine had written a bestseller entitled *Your Inner Child of the Past.* I had read it in the '70s, but, of course, it had nothing to do with me. Even then, the inner child concept was not as deeply explored as it became later, primarily by John Bradshaw.

As I progressed across my Bridge of Recovery, I thought more and more about my inner child. Was there actually such a creature? Since my early teens, I had heard a screaming voice within. I assumed that everyone had this screaming voice. Now I wondered. Could that be my inner child? About two years before I entered recovery, I purchased a doll with no face. I had no way of knowing that my desire to have one without a face was because I couldn't see the real me. Halfway through recovery, as the light at the end of that bridge became visible, I searched for a doll with a face. I found her at an arts and crafts festival. Not only did she have a face, but it was a happy one. When I turned her over and wound the key on her back, she played, "We've only just begun." I'd found the symbol I needed to begin exploring my inner self for that child.

One day, as I sat on a swing in a nearby park, I spoke out loud to my imaginary child. I wasn't sure I believed in her, but the doll on my bed haunted me. What if there were a child? What if she were waiting for me to reach out and comfort her? Hesitantly, I continued speaking. I told her I was sorry I had put her through so much. I apologized for not listening to the screaming voice. I said, in almost a whisper, that I was working on getting well, and I promised that one day she would no longer scream, she would no longer cry, she would be the happy face. All of a sudden, I felt as if a little girl had stepped out of the shadows, her tear-stained face staring up at me. I began sobbing and literally reached down and wrapped my arms around her as we both wept.

During the next few months, I spent many mornings at that park while we swung together. She told me about the time the bullies in the schoolyard had thrown rocks at her for what she was wearing. I consoled her about the loss of her first love in the fifth grade, a boy named Jerry Bennett. From there, we grieved over the loss of her mother, the loneliness and despair of her teen years, the scars of her siblings, and the early and tragic death of her baby sister. Together, we explored all the moments, and as the months continued to pass, she stopped crying, stopped wearing a mournful look, and after my recovery ended, laughed and played. Today, my inner child and I connect immediately whenever I am involved in activities she likes best—swinging on swings, sliding down slides, climbing trees, and hiking in the woods, all activities that, despite being the grandmother of thirteen and the great-grandmother of eight, I do with relish.

As you move through recovery, you will find your inner child growing emotionally as a new-found maturity develops in both of you. The frightened child you once were becomes an adult who is capable of being child-like, but not childish. This change brings great inner strength.

The concept of this inner child may seem silly to you as it once did to me. But she is very real in each one of you. She is that innocent child before the time of trauma. She is waiting for you to begin recovery, to rescue her from that dark place where she has lived for so many years. Don't turn your back on her. I promise that once you reach the other side of the bridge, your joy in life will be overwhelming.

To enhance the happy ending to my story, in 1995, my oldest daughter, Cathy, committed herself to an addictive disorder center for thirty days for alcoholism. A year later, Cathy and her husband had Emily Rose, the first child in my family to be born to a treated victim of childhood sexual abuse. In October of 2014, Cathy celebrated nineteen years of sobriety.

As time passed and I made wiser choices, I also saw a pronounced difference in the choices my other daughters made. Although they are not yet in recovery, both have rid themselves of their abusers. As you can see, a treated incest victim can influence the lives of her children a great deal. Today, I see them making positive changes and mature decisions, and for the first time since they became adults, my daughters are leading happier lives.

As for me, my days are rich and filled with joy. In May of 2000, I married another McKinnon, a mountain man named Tom from the Colorado Rockies whom I met through the Internet during a genealogy search. We were married at Melrose Abbey in Melrose, Scotland, with bagpipers playing at a reception that included a number of friends we've made from the United Kingdom. Tom is gentle, kind, full of personal integrity, and cherishes me as I deserve. Today, we live near Sedona, Arizona, a dream I'd had for many years.

Chuck, the man who died of cancer, and I have three grandchildren together, two of them born after his death. I had promised him before he died that I would tell his grandchildren about him so they would know him as I did. Until I moved to Colorado, every year on the anniversary of his birthday, Michael, Hunter, and Katie Montana wrote letters to the grandfather they never knew. Together, we visited his grave, where they put flowers on his headstone and read to him the letters they'd written. Wherever Chuck is, I feel he has forgiven me as I have forgiven myself.

Chapter 7

Things That Go Bump in the Night

The Biology of Stress and Trauma

Robin Karr-Morse

F OR MOST OF US, fear is a double-edged sword. Fueling forms of entertainment ranging from reality television to media coverage of daily news, to race-car driving, to amusement park rides, violent movies and video games, fear induction is a hot commodity—at least in measured doses. Instinctively, we are captured, challenged, intrigued, motivated—and sometimes paralyzed—by this primal emotion. While essential to our survival, fear can also—if overstimulated—become the unintended emissary of death. It's not surprising, then, that many of us have a love hate relationship with fear. Throughout history, political systems have harnessed and manipulated this aspect of human nature at least as effectively as today's producers of reality television.

Under less threatening and more controlled circumstances, fear provides a source of thrills, energy and enhanced learning. Most of us can easily remember how fear of losing the game or failing the test delivers the rush that fuels the win or the high score. Fear can be exhilarating, as in extreme sports like mountain climbing and surfing giant waves. It can also crystallize moments in memory, especially those recorded with deeply engraved emotions, some of which we wish we could erase. In our earliest lives, even before we mastered words or reason, we may have stored adrenaline-etched memories in our primitive brains from a single searing experience, such as avoiding a snarling dog or pulling little fingers away from a flame. These lessons were indelibly recorded in our memories precisely because they were essential to surviving the uniquely prolonged dependency and vulnerability that characterize human childhood.

FEAR AND ITS MINIONS

In *Scared Sick*, "fear" is defined as our most fundamental emotional and physical response to a perceived threat, triggering the chain of physical responses commonly known as *fight-or-flight*. Fear is recognizable in all animals, even in rodents. Rats freeze on the spot, immediately ceasing exploration and investigation. Humans are subtler, but not by much. We hold our breath, our hearts race, and both our blood pressure and muscle tone increase. We may break out in a cold sweat. In extreme cases, as when we have experienced abuse as children or have grown up in the wake of disasters such as war, ethnic cleansing or famine, our brains become permanently wired for survival in a dangerous world. Ironically, the very defenses developed to protect us under dangerous circumstances may become a huge liability in later, less-threatening chapters of our lives, especially if these defenses are now triggered without conscious awareness or control.

So, for example, the child who is constantly ridiculed or shamed or hit by an alcoholic parent and who develops extreme hypervigilance and readiness to fight at any provocation may appear aggressive, hostile, even paranoid in a less-threatening environment like school. Or a child rendered powerless in the face of adult aggression may appear frozen, depressed and abnormally passive, even self-destructive, with unfamiliar adults outside the home.

But without our adrenaline-driven alarm system, the fight-or-flight response—or more accurately, the *fight-flight-freeze* response—we would be in constant peril. When, for example, we see a snake in the grass or a swarm of yellow jackets coming for us, this is the system that enables input from the senses to instantaneously signal large muscles in the arms or legs to fight or flee, bypassing the normally slower route through the analytical brain. When there is no time for analysis, no time for deliberations concerning the perceived threat, our brain has an emergency route directly to the alarm center, the amygdala, so that in a nanosecond our entire body is activated in fight or flight. Our brain is so good at this instantaneous preparation that associated sensual information—sights, smells, sounds, recorded at the same time—can trigger fight-or-flight before we are consciously aware of the threat. But when we are helpless, like a small child in the face of a violent assault by an adult, we can neither fight nor flee. In the wake of overwhelming fear, we enter a state known as *freeze*. In the animal kingdom, freeze imitates death, allowing an animal to escape a predator. For humans, freeze works differently. We become emotionally numb, removed from reality.

The problem is that fight-flight-freeze, which originally evolved to protect us in the face of an occasional acute physical danger—like an attack from a wild beast—has not adapted to the challenges of life in the twenty-first century. Acute physical threats are no longer our primary threats. In Western culture, for example, the need to hunt for our next meal has been replaced by the need to drive on crowded freeways to stores and offices, to make money to purchase necessities, and to interface with all kinds of people, often at a merciless pace set by the technologies that now rule our lives. Having evolved as hunter-gatherers in small mobile communities close to the land, we now find ourselves living mostly in densely populated areas in constant proximity to strangers, often with little connection to the natural environment. For most of us, challenges have shifted from immediate physical threats to chronic emotional ones. To the degree that the realities of modern living—including staggering advances in technology, increasing population density and drastic changes in our roles and relationships with other humans—have outpaced the adaptations of our internal physical systems, we experience what we call *stress*. To top it all off, we are the only species, as far as we know, that worries, projecting concerns into the future and ruminating on our fears, which keeps the stress cycle running overtime.

Ephemeral sensations we call "feelings"—our emotions—fuel the stress response. In fact, our feelings, often disguised, repressed or denied, are in constant chemical communication with our brains—and consequently with all key systems in our bodies—about the status of our health and safety. When we experience a feeling of overwhelming fear, our bodies reflect critical changes in the systems designed to protect life. We are often confused about the identity of negative feelings: "What is this sensation in my gut (or my shoulders, or temples)?" "Is this anger or frustration?" "Am I anxious or depressed, exhausted or sad?" What most of us know for sure when we are "stressed" is that we experience "dis-ease." We know that we are not at ease, that we are uncomfortable; there is both clarity and irony in this term.

Most of us know the feeling of being moderately stressed, however overused and non-specific that term may be. "Being stressed" is commonly used to denote a vague, unpleasant sense of feeling off balance emotionally or physically. Originally an architectural or engineering term to describe the pressure on structures that might cause them to break, "stress" has become a generic term that we commonly use instead of specifically describing feelings as varied as frustration, exhaustion, anxiety, distraction, fear, embarrassment and anger. When we say we are "stressed out," we might mean that we are fighting with a partner, or feeling overwhelmed by work or kids or school, or exhausted by too many demands and too little time. Regardless of vague descriptions, these negative feelings are registering in our bodies—for better or worse—chemically and organically. And extreme stress is measurable in physical terms: degree of abdominal fat, waist-hip ratio, baseline blood pressure and measures of our overnight production of cortisol or adrenaline.

In *Scared Sick*, we use the term *stressor* in reference to an external event *outside* of our bodies that results in the negative emotions and accompanying physical sensations *inside* our bodies that we call "stress." Not all stress is harmful. We experience some stress getting up in the morning, or going to school or work. For a child, receiving an immunization, going to the dentist, or getting a haircut are typical stressors with positive outcomes for the child. Some stress is essential—for example, scheduling and arriving on time for appointments, taking tests, or going for physical examinations. Researchers refer to this type of stress as *positive stress*. Positive stress actually improves immune function and facilitates an effective response to more serious stressors in much the same way that short regular sprints prepare us for the marathon. It sharpens our attention and enables us to remember life-protecting information like a mistake in judgment that we don't want to repeat. It heightens acute sensual focus. Think of driving alone at night on an icy road. It is stress—the fight-or-flight response—that heightens our alertness, sharpens our senses, and speeds our responses to the sheen on the road or the slip of a tire that indicates danger. Brief episodes of stress are what our stress systems are designed for and may actually be better for us than no stress at all.

A second category of stress is *tolerable stress*. This is stress that could become harmful, like getting divorced, having a parent or partner die, or losing a job. The capacity to recover is what keeps tolerable stress from becoming *toxic stress*—or trauma. Under tolerable stress, we have access to the healing process through relationships with friends, family or professionals and practices like regular exercise, meditation, healthful eating, adequate sleep and personal time to regroup. Though we are still affected by stress, we are able to regain internal balance or what researchers call *homeostasis*—a healthy balance within our central nervous, immune and endocrine systems that protects health. Being able to trust, to talk openly, to be heard empathically, to physically release stress through dancing or running or swimming or drumming—these are critical elements in preventing tolerable stress from turning into toxic stress.

Toxic stress is the problem. When it is strong, frequent or prolonged by emotional experiences that overwhelm homeostasis, toxic stress triggers the freeze response. In the grip of toxic stress, we don't fully regain our former equilibrium because the healing relationships and practices that may have worked with tolerable stress are now inaccessible, insufficient or unsuccessful. If it continues and accumulates in our bodies, toxic stress dysregulates the systems that protect health, paving the way for disease.

HOMELAND SECURITY

We all know the feeling: our blood pressure and breathing increase to mount the battle, our muscles tighten so we can run faster, leap farther or hit harder, and our senses go on red alert so we can see and hear more acutely. And as soon as the danger passes, we return to normal— collapsing or breathing a sigh of relief.

This is the normal response when one form of stress or another triggers the HPA axis: the relationship among the hypothalamus (H), the pituitary gland (P) and the adrenal glands (A) that produces finely tuned chemical messages that connect the central nervous, endocrine and immune systems. HPA is the linchpin that activates the body's main defenses. Together these three systems are the sentinels of health, functioning like internal radar. Constantly responsive to internal and external threats—from germs to terrorists—the systems of the HPA axis marshal the troops to defeat the threat, then resume their posts.

Dr. Bruce McEwen, professor of neuroendocrinology at Rockefeller University in New York and a prolific researcher on the subject, views stress as any physical or emotional challenge to the major systems of the body. He points out that the interactive nature of the three systems that comprise the HPA axis and their capacity to communicate and adjust to varying conditions have enabled humans to prevail through evolutionary challenges such as extreme climate changes, varying geographical terrains and variations in available foods. These systems work like an integrated thermostat, sending chemical messages back and forth to maintain homeostasis in response to changing conditions—especially anything that is life-threatening. Through a mutually regulatory system of lending and borrowing, activating and deactivating vital chemical messengers, they prepare the body for any perceived threat. Their job is to sustain life at all costs.

McEwen calls the HPA axis–driven process *allostasis*. This capacity to respond to a threat and return to homeostasis is essential. In healthy people, allostasis occurs almost automatically, frequently and expediently after normal physical stressors like running, chasing a ball or climbing a set of stairs. Allostasis also kicks in under everyday emotional stresses, such as giving a report in school or taking a driver's test. But problems arise when intense stressors come at us so frequently that allostasis can't fully shut down the stress response or when we need the activating energy of the stress response and allostasis doesn't shift into gear.

To imagine how allostasis works, picture a temperature gauge on the dashboard of a car. When the engine is functioning within the normal range for which it is designed, the needle stays in a green area left of center on the gauge. But if the engine overheats, the needle goes into a red area right of center, indicating alarm. Our stress response system works similarly. When we are stressed, allostasis quickly sends our HPA into the "red zone." As soon as the threat has passed, allostasis sends our alarm system right back down into the "green zone," where it is meant to function. But if the stress response is stimulated over and over without much respite, toxic stress can wear this system down so that our HPA doesn't fully return to the green zone and stay there. With chronic overstimulation, the resting state of the HPA system gradually climbs to a higher and higher default, edging toward and then staying in the red zone. Eventually it may remain there, never fully recovering its original balance.

McEwen uses the term *allostatic load* to refer to the wear and tear on the body from the overuse of allostasis and the consequent dysregulation of affected systems. When stressful conditions continue and accumulate without repair over time—or even when we neglect healthy balancing practices, like getting adequate exercise—our allostatic load will ramp up. Those of us who live in a family where there is continual conflict or fear, in a war zone, or in a violent neighborhood, or if we live in poverty or in a disaster zone—like the Japanese after the earthquake, tsunami and nuclear catastrophe of March 2011—we are at risk of chronic stress, a reality recognized by health professionals and researchers for some time.

But the surprising news is that people who experience low levels of constant annoyance every day, such as frustrating, boring or demeaning jobs, are also at risk. McEwen tells the story of workers on an assembly line at a Volvo factory in Sweden who were demoralized and miserable from doing the same job over and over. As measured by blood cortisol levels, waist-hip fat ratios and production of adrenaline, their stress levels were high. When the factory reorganized so that everyone worked on teams and on a variety of tasks, stress levels declined.[1]

McEwen believes that chronic stress is toxic stress and that it causes problems with memory, premature aging and overstimulation of nerve cells. It often leads to the loss of tissue in key parts of the brain, especially the memory center, and to dysregulation of normally protective response systems, such as the immune response. Cortisol, the hormone produced by the adrenals, calms the system and enables it to return to homeo-stasis, signaling the immune system that all is well. Over time *hyper*-arousal may lead to a state of *hypo*-arousal (under-arousal) as adrenal glands become exhausted and cortisol decreases. When cortisol is depleted, overactive immune responses may attack normal processes and tissues, resulting in autoimmune conditions like lupus, various allergies or chronic fatigue syndrome.

Chronic stressors are likely to be the culprits at the root of many diseases. We are espe-cially vulnerable to chronic negative emotions (fear, anger, shame, guilt, embarrassment, grief) when we are young, particularly if we were exposed to prenatal stress. And the gloomy news is that those of us exposed early become more—not less—vulnerable to the effects of chronic stress as we age, which in turn contributes to cognitive impairment and dementia. When high levels of stress, especially worry, continue into later life, they can cause shrinkage to the hippocampus in the aging brain, reducing memory and increasing the risk of Alzheimer's. One Montreal study showed that the hippocampi of older people whose stress hormones rose over a five-year period were 14 percent smaller than in people of the same age whose stress hormones were not elevated. The former group had difficulty remembering lists of words and paragraphs and negotiating mazes—symptoms predictive of increased risk of Alzheimer's and diabetes.[2] While researchers have long known that trauma appears to contribute to the accumulation of the neurofibrillary tangles that are characteristic of Alzheimer's, they now suspect that excessive HPA stimulation in everyday stress may contribute to the disease as well.[3] So there is good reason, regardless of our age, to begin lowering stress levels; the advantages of doing so only continue to increase as we mature!

TRAUMA: FROZEN FEAR

At the farthest end of the fear spectrum is emotional *trauma*, which occurs when we are faced with either a single overwhelming event or a "last straw" in an accumulation of experiences over which we feel we have no control. Trauma is an extreme form of fear accompanied by a state of perceived helplessness—and often hopelessness. Although we tend to think of trauma as a huge event, like an automobile accident or the death of a loved one, here we use a definition similar to that of writer Annie Rogers, who defines trauma as any experience that "by its nature is in excess of what we can manage or bear."[4] Thus, when fight-or-flight, our first response to stress, fails or is unavailable, we move into the freeze response, the defining sign of trauma. In this book, "trauma" is used interchangeably with "terror" and "shock." The central difference between toxic stress and trauma is that *trauma always triggers the freeze response.* When we are unable to fight or flee, freezing is the only option left.

Trauma may not appear horrific to the onlooker. It may be subtle and quiet, and to anyone who asks, we who have been traumatized may say that we are "fine." But following trauma, our look is typically one of shock, and the state we are in is called *dissociation*.

From the inside looking out, we are emotionally numb, perceiving our surroundings through a fragmented and distorted lens. Unable to respond to normal conversation with any real focus on the content, our responses may seem abstract. We may act in a rote, mechanistic manner without spontaneous affect, or suddenly erupt violently. Some victims of trauma seem amnesiac. One client whom I saw shortly after her husband's suicide (he shot himself in their home while she went for groceries) was preoccupied about the water heater that had flooded in the same room and fretful about how she was going to handle that. She was a very bright and organized thinker but appeared unfocused and repeatedly assured me she was "fine."

Immediately after experiencing trauma, most of us will find it hard to express ourselves in words; what we say may not reflect our normal range of analysis, and we may not remember what we just said. This is the impact of the internal chemistry of trauma—nature's temporary but effective anesthetic that renders us unable to feel the impact of the event, insulated from the here and now. We are in a "fog"—a state in which normal rational thinking and emotional and physical pain are temporarily suspended.

Both toxic stress and trauma trigger the same initial biological response: the HPA axis. But when trauma occurs, the energy that would normally be dispersed through fleeing or fighting is trapped. The systems in the body being primed for action are simultaneously blocked from discharging that energy, and the result is a cavalcade of maladaptations in the immune and endocrine systems. Rather than discharging the energy that accompanies fight-or-flight and returning to balance or homeostasis, two systems in the body are now at war with each other. One system activates the body with chemical signals of alarm. A second system is trying to counter this by secreting cortisol to gentle the fight-flight activation. Disease can result from the overproduction of hormones by either system. Exactly how this renders any one of us sick, emotionally or physically, depends on our genetics, prior experiences, our interpretation of the experience and the availability of support.

We are learning more about this daily. For most of human history a live look at the brain was available only through animal studies; autopsy afforded our only opportunity in humans. But new technologies in the last two decades have provided clear images of the actively functioning brain in real time. Positron-emission tomography (PET), single photon emission computed tomography (SPECT) and functional magnetic resonance imaging (MRI) allow us to see still crude but graphic changes in the brains of individuals diagnosed with post-traumatic stress disorder (PTSD). The clearest currently discerned difference is shrinkage in the hippocampus, likely resulting from excessive cortisol.

When it comes to trauma, physical and emotional are inseparable. What happens to us emotionally happens to us physically, and vice versa. And while stress and trauma are on the same continuum, they are not the same thing. Stress is a normal response to feeling threatened or overwhelmed. Trauma, on the other hand, is toxic stress frozen into place in our brains and bodies, where it reverberates chemically, generating tiny pathological shifts in immune and endocrine functions. According to a website devoted to healing trauma: "If we can communicate our distress to people who care about us and can respond adequately, we are in the realm of stress. If we become frozen in a state of active emotional intensity, we are experiencing an emotional trauma—even though we may not be consciously aware of the level of distress we are experiencing."[5]

Trauma—especially for children who have not yet learned language— tends to be stored in the brain not primarily as a conscious, rational, language-based experience in *declarative memory* but rather as a somatic or "feeling" memory stored in unconscious or *procedural memory*. Somatic memories may surface later in life in the form of physical symptoms that seem to have no discernible cause, such as chronic pain, headache or fibromyalgia.

ANXIETY: THE SHADOW OF FEAR

Humans are the only species that can develop emotional pathology based on stress because we are the only species whose advanced brains allow us to keep stressors actively present in our minds. A lingering low level of fear known as worry or *anxiety* keeps stressors alive in our minds and consequently in our bodies. Anxiety or worry—essentially the same processes—are the shadows of fear, a feeling that lingers long after the initial threat has passed or that looms long before the anticipated event. We can't stop thinking about the exam next week, or the job interview, the mistake we made, the deadline, or the possible surgery. Even when it's over, we still can't relax.

Over time, chronic anxiety may grow from being a state—an immediate but passing sensation—to being a trait, a persistent way of being. Anxiety can suspend an individual in pervasive low-grade fight-flight limbo, potentially triggering panic attacks and numerous physical conditions.

There is little question that some of us are more prone to anxiety than others. The degree of our reactivity to various stressors and the degree to which the emotion of fear can trigger or aggravate disease may be determined in part by genetics; inborn temperament seems to be a major player in the equation. But increasingly, early experience is being credited with playing an equivalent if not stronger role. Many researchers believe that "inborn" temperament is itself greatly influenced by experiences in the womb that shape who we become, anxious or otherwise.[6]

Focusing on this question of the genetic roots of anxiety, Kenneth Kendler, a psychiatric geneticist at Virginia Commonwealth University in Richmond, turned to identical twins—who share all their genes—and compared them with fraternal twins, who share only some. Kendler found that while identical twins are slightly more likely to be similar than fraternal twins in their degree of anxiety (measured as generalized anxiety disorder, panic attacks and phobias), the overall likelihood of heritability of these disorders was only in the moderate range (30 to 40 percent). He believes that our upbringing and experiences are the pivotal factors in determining our tendency toward anxiety.[7]

NOTES

1   Dr. Bruce S. McEwen, interview with the authors, New York City, April 23, 2008.

2   B. S. McEwen and E. Norton, The End of Stress as We Know It, Washington, D.C.: National Academies Press, 2002.

3   Salk Institute, "Possible Mechanistic Link Between Stress and the Development of Alzheimer Tangles," ScienceDaily, June 15, 2007, available at: http://www.sciencedaily .com/releases/2007/06/070614155344.htm (accessed July 14, 2010).

4   A. Rogers, The Hidden Language of Trauma, New York: Random House, 2006.

5   Santa Barbara Graduate Institute Center for Clinical Studies and Research and Los Angeles County Early Identification and Intervention Group, "Emotional and Psychological Trauma: Causes and Effects, Symptoms and Treatment," reprinted from Helpguide.org, 2005, available at: http://www.healingresources.info/emotional_trauma _overview.htm.

6   M. J. Meaney, S. Bhatnagar, S. Larocque, et al., "Early Environment and the Development of Individual Differences in the Hypothalamic-Pituitary-Adrenal Stress Response," in Severe Stress and Mental Disturbance in Children, ed. C. R. Pfeffer, Washington, D.C.: American Psychiatric Press, 1996, 85–131.

7   C. Gorman, "The Science of Anxiety: Why Do We Worry Ourselves Sick? Because the Brain Is Hardwired for Fear, and Sometimes It Short-Circuits," Time, June 10, 2002, 46–54.

References

American Psychological Association. (APA). (2016). *Protecting our children from abuse and neglect.* Retrieved from www.apa.org/pi/families/resources/abuse.aspx

American Society for the Prevention of Cruelty to Children (American SPCC). (2018). *Emotional child abuse?* Retrieved from https://americanspcc.org/emotional-child-abuse/

American SPCC. (n.d.) *Neglect of a child.* Retrieved from http://americanspcc.org/neglect/

American SPCC. (n.d.). *Child sexual abuse facts.* Retrieved from http://americanspcc.org/indicators-child-abuse/

American SPCC. (n.d.). *Child abuse statistics.* Retrieved from http://americanspcc.org/child-abuse-statistics/

American SPCC. (n.d.). *Emotional child abuse.* Retrieved from http://americanspcc.org/emotional-child-abuse

American SPCC (n.d.). *Statistics and facts about child abuse in the U. S.* Retrieved from http://americanspcc.org/child-abuse-statistics/

American SPCC. (n.d.). *What is child sexual abuse.* Retrieved from http://americanspcc.org/child-sexual-abuse/

Anda, R., Felitti, V., Bremner, J., Douglas, W. J., Whitfield, C., Perry, B.D., Dube, S. and Giles, W. (2006). The enduring effects of abuse and related adverse experiences in childhood: A convergence of evidence from neurobiology and epidemiology. *Eur. ArchPsychiatry Clinical Neuroscience* (2006), 256, 174–186

Babbel, S. (2013, March 12). *Trauma: Childhood sexual abuse.* Retrieved from https://www.psychologytoday.com/blog/somatic-psychology/201303/trauma-childhood-sexual-abuse

Babbel, S. (2011, April 24). *The lingering trauma of child abuse.* Retrieved from https://www.psychologytoday.com/Blog/somatic-psychology/201104/the-lingering-trauma-child-abuse/

Bailey, E. (2013) *Hyperarousal.* Retrieved fromhttp://www.healthcentral.com/anxiety/c/1443/159977/hyperarousal/

Bancroft, S. (1997). Becoming heroes: Teachers can help abused children. *Educational Leadership,* 55(2), 69–71.

Bear, T., Schenk, S., & Buckner, L. (1992/1993). Supporting victims of child abuse. *Educational Leadership.* 50(4), 42-47.

Berliner, L., & Conte, J. R. (1990). *The process of victimization: the victims' perspective*. Child Abuse and Neglect, 14, 29–40. Retrieved from http://psycnet.apa.org/record/1990-19953-001

Carlson, E. & Ruzek, J. (2001) in Magellan Health Services, Inc. *Wellness tips…Traumatic experiences*. Retrieved from https://legacy.jdeckman.com:8888/Portals/0/Effects%20of%20Traumatic%20Events%20-%20Final.pdf

Centers for Disease Control. (2016). *ACE study*. Retrieved from https://www.cdc.gov/violenceprevention/acestudy/index.html

Centers for Disease Control and Prevention (n.d.). *Violence prevention in ACE study*. Retrieved from http://www.cdc.gov/violenceprevention/acestudy/index.html

CDC. (2016). *Child abuse and neglect: Consequences*. Retrieved from http://www.cdc.gov/violenceprevention/childmaltreatment/consequences.html

Child Information Gateway (2011, July). *Child maltreatment prevention: Past, present and future*. Washington, DC: U.S. Department of Health and Human Services, Children's Bureau.

Child Information Gateway (2011, August). *Supporting brain development in traumatized children and youth*. DC: U.S. Department of Health and Human Services, Children's Bureau.

Child Information Gateway (2012). *The risk and prevention of maltreatment of children with disabilities*. Washington, DC: U.S. Department of Health and Human Services,Children's Bureau.

Child Information Gateway (2015). *Trends and numbers*. Washington, DC: U.S. Department of Health and Human Services, Children's Bureau.

Child Information Gateway (2012, March). *The risk and prevention of maltreatment of children with disabilities*. Washington, DC: U.S. Department of Health and Human Services, Children's Bureau.Child Information Gateway (2012, August). Acts of omission: An overview of child neglect.Washington, DC: U.S. Department of Health and Human Services, Children's Bureau.

Child Information Gateway (2012, 2014). *Child maltreatment report with disabilities*.
Washington, DC: U.S. Department of Health and Human Services, Children's Bureau.

Child Information Gateway (2013, July). *Long term consequences of child abuse and neglect*. Washington, DC: U.S. Department of Health and Human Services, Children's Bureau.

Child Information Gateway (2013, July). What is child abuse and neglect? *Recognizing the signs and symptoms*. Washington, DC: U.S. Department of Health and Human Services, Children's Bureau.

Child Information Gateway (2013, November). *Mandatory reporters of child abuse and neglect, state statutes through November 2013*. Washington, DC: U.S. Department of Health and Human Services, Children's Bureau.

Child Information Gateway (April 2015). *Child abuse and neglect fatalities 2013*. Washington, DC: U.S. Department of Health and Human Services, Children's Bureau.

Child Welfare Information Gateway. (2007). *Definitions of child abuse and neglect: Summary of state laws*. Washington, DC: US Department of Health and Human Services Administration for Children and Families. Retrieved from: http://www.childwelfare.gov/ systemwide/ laws_policies/statutes/defineall.pdf

Child Welfare Information Gateway. (2015). Washington, DC: U.S. Department of Health and Human Services, Children's Bureau. *State statutes*. Retrieved from https://www.childwelfare.

gov/topics/systemwide/laws-policies/state/?CWIGFunctionsaction=statestatutes:main.
getResults

Child Witness to Violence Project. (n.d.). *Understand the problem.* Retrieved from www.child-witnesstoviolence.org

Childhelp. (n.d.). *Child abuse statistics & facts.* Retrieved from www.childhelp.org/child-abuse-statistics/

Crosson-Tower, C. (2003). *The role of educators in preventing and responding to child abuse and neglect.* In Child abuse and neglect user manual series. Child Welfare Information Gateway. Department of Health and Human Services, Children's Bureau. Retrieved from https://www.childwelfare.gov/pubPDFs/educator.pdf

Crosson-Tower, C. (2005). *Understanding child abuse and neglect* (3rd ed.). Boston, MA: Pearson

Davies, L. (n.d.). *Helping the sexually abused child.* Retrieved from http://www.kellybear.com/TeacherArticles/TeacherTip10.html

DoSomething. (n.d.). *11 facts about child abuse.* Retrieved from https://www.dosomething.org/us/facts/11-facts-about-child-abuse

Emotional maltreatment (n.d.). Retrieved from http://americanspcc.org/emotional-child-abuse/

Every Child Matters. (n.d.). *Prevent child abuse & end deaths from abuse and neglect.* Retrieved from http://everychildmatters.org/our-issues/safe-kids/

Every Child Matters. (2012, July). *Child abuse & neglect deaths in America.* Retrieved from http://everychildmatters.org/

Facts & myths (n.d.). Retrieved from http://www.childwitnesstoviolence.org/facts--myths.html
Family Nurturing Center. (2002). *What every teacher needs to know about child abuse: A resource guide for educators and school personnel.* Retrieved from www.familynurture.org

FindLaw. (2018). *Child abuse background and history.* Retrieved from http://family.findlaw.com/child-abuse/child-abuse-background-and-history.html

Florida Institute of Technology Family Learning Program, (n.d.) *Information about sexual abuse.* Retrieved from https://research.fit.edu/flp/information-about-sexual-abuse/

Gershoff, E.T. (2008). *Report on physical punishment in the U.S.: What research tells us about its effects on children.* Columbus, OH: Center for Effective Discipline. Retrieved from http://www.phoenixchildrens.com/PDFs/principles_and_practices-of_effective_ discipline.pdf

Glaser, D. (2000). Child abuse and neglect and the brain — A review. *Journal of Child Psychology and Psychiatry.* 41(1), 97–116.

Grogan-Kaylor, A. (2004). The effect of corporal punishment on anti-social behavior in children. *Social Work Research*, 28, 153–162

Helpguide.org. (n.d.). *PTSD – trauma.* Retrieved from https://www.helpguide.org/home-pages/ptsd-trauma.htm

Helpguide.org. (2018). *Recognizing, preventing and reporting child abuse.* Retrieved from http://www.helpguide.org/articles/abuse/child-abuse-and-neglect.htm

Helping the abused student in the classroom (n.d.). Retrieved from http://www.secasa.com.au/pages/helping-the-abused-student-in-this-classroom/

Henderson, T.A. (1992). *The BASER model*. As cited in *FIT Family Learning Program Information about sexual abuse*. Retrieved from https://research.fit.edu/flp/information-about-sexual-abuse/

Hendrikson, H. & Blackman, K. (2015, August). State policies addressing child abuse and neglect. Retrieved from http://www.ncsl.org/Portals/1/Documents/Health/StatePolicies_ChildAbuse.pdf

Hopper, J. (n.d.). *Unwanted or abusive childhood experiences*. Retrieved fromwww.jimhopper.com/abstats/#s-intro

Hyperarousal. (n.d.) *Dorland's Medical Dictionary for Health Consumers*. (2007). Retrieved July 12 2018 from https://medical-dictionary.thefreedictionary.com/hyperarousal

Indicators of child abuse/neglect (n.d.). Retrieved fromhttp://americanspcc.org/indicators-child-abuse/

Information about sexual abuse (n.d.). Retrieved from http://research.fit.edu/flp/info-sexual-abuse-php

Information by State (n.d.). Retrieved from http://family.findlaw.com/child-abuse/child-abuse-information-by-state.html

Jaudes, P.K., & Mackey-Bilaver, L. (2008). Do chronic conditions increase young children's risk of being maltreated? *Child Abuse and Neglect: The International Journal*. 32(3), 671–681.

Joyful Heart Foundation. (n.d.). *Developmental and psychological effects of child abuse and neglect*. Retrieved from http://www.joyfulheartfoundation.org/learn/child-abuse-neglect/effects-child-abuse-neglect

Kids Matter, Inc. (2016). *Child sexual abuse*. Retrieved from https://www.kidsmatterinc.org/get-help/for-families/abuse-and-neglect/child-sexual-abuse/

Kids Matter, Inc. (n.d.). *Reporting child abuse*. Retrieved from www.kidsmatterinc.org/get-help/child-welfare-agencies/reporting-child-abuse/

McLeod, S.A. (2013). *Erik Erikson*. Retrieved from www.simplypsychology.org/Erik-Erikson.html

Myers, J. (2008). A short history of child protection in America. *Family Law Quarterly*, 42(3), pp. 449-463.

National Center for Children in Poverty (NCCP). (n.d.). *Child poverty*. Retrieved from http://www.nccp.org/topics/childpoverty.html

National Child Traumatic Stress Network, Physical Abuse Collaborative Group (2009). *Physical punishment: What parents should know*. Los Angeles, CA: National Center for Child Traumatic Stress.

National Child Traumatic Stress, Network, Physical Abuse Collaborative Group (2009). *Child physical abuse fact sheet*. Los Angeles, CA: National Center for Child Traumatic Stress.

National Children's Alliance (2014). *National children's alliance statistical fact sheet, national children's alliance 2013 and 2014 national statistics*. Retrieved from http://www.nationalchildrensalliance.org/cac-statistics

NCSL. (2011). *Child abuse and neglect reporting statutes*. Retrieved from http://www.ncsl.org/research/human-services/child-abuse-and-neglect-reporting-statutes.aspx

Nebraska Department of Veterans' Affairs. (2007). *Post-traumatic stress disorder.* Retrieved from http://www.ptsd.ne.gov/what-is-ptsd.html

Nebraska Department of Veterans' Affairs. (2007). *What is PTSD?* Retrieved from http://www.ptsd.ne.gov/what-is-ptsd.html

New York State Office of Child and Family Services. (2018). *Summary guide for mandated reporters in New York State.* Retrieved from https://ocfs.ny.gov/main/publications/pub1159.pdf

New York State Office of Child and Family Services. (n.d.). *Frequently asked questions.* Retrieved from https://ocfs.ny.gov/main/cps/faqs.asp

Orelove, F. P., Hollahan, D.J., & Miles, K. T. (2000). Maltreatment of children with disabilities: Training needs for a collaborative response. *Child Abuse & Neglect, 24*(2), 185-194.

Petit, M. (2011, October 17). *Why child abuse is so acute in the US.* Retrieved from http://www.bbc.co.uk/news/magazine-15193530

Perry, B. (n.d.). *Principles of working with traumatized children.* Retrieved from http://teacher.scholastic.com/professional/brueperry/working_children.htm

Perry, B. D. (2003). *Effects of traumatic events on children.* Retrieved from www.ChildTrauma.org Policy Guidelines (n.d.), Retrieved from https://www2.ed.gov/policy/speced/guid/edpicks.jhtml?src=ln

Prevent Child Abuse NY. (2009, July). *Identifying and reporting child abuse and neglect: A mandated reporter handbook.* Retrieved from www.preventchildabuseny.org /resour/about-child-abuse

Prevent Child Abuse NY. (2010). *Child abuse and neglect fact sheet.* Retrieved from www.preventchildabuseny.org

Prevent Child Abuse New York. Child Abuse & Neglect (1998). 22(2), 79-90. Retrieved from https://www.preventchildabuseny.org/resour

Prevent Child Abuse NY. (n.d.). *Defining and recognizing child abuse.* Retrieved from http://preventchildabuseny.org/resources/about-child-abuse/

Prevent Child Abuse America. (2016). *Recognizing child abuse: What parents should know.* Retrieved from http://preventchildabuse.org/resource/recognizing-child-abuse-what-parents-should-%20know/

Post-traumatic stress disorder (ptsd): Symptoms, treatment and self-help for ptsd (n.d.). Retrieved from http://www.helpguide.org/articles/ptsd-trauma/post-traumatic-stress- -disorder.htm

PTSD in children and adolescents (n.d.). Retrieved from https://www.ptsd.va.gov/professional/treatment/children/ptsd_in_children_and_adolescents_overview_for_professionals.asp

Ramamoorthy, S. and Myers-Walls, J. (n.d.). *Talking to a child who has been abused.* Retrieved from www.extension/purdue.edu/providerparent/parent-provider

RAINN. (2016). *What is child sexual abuse.* Retrieved from https://www.rainn.org/articles/child-sexual-abuse

RAINN. (n.d.). *If you suspect a child is being harmed.* Retrieved from https://rainn.org/get-information/types-of-sexual-assault/incest

Recognizing & reporting child abuse & neglect (n.d.). Retrieved from www.nyc.gov/acs

Reporting child abuse and neglect: Mandatory reporting facts (n.d.). Retrieved fromhttp://teaching.monster.com/benefits/articles/1929-reporting-child-abuse-and-neglect-mandatory-reporting-facts

SafeHorizon. (n.d.). *10 signs of child abuse*. Retrieved from https://www.safehorizon.org/get-help/child-abuse/

Sedlak, A.J., Mettenburg, J., Basena, M., Petta, I., McPherson, K., Greene, A., and Li, S. (2010). Fourth National Incidence Study of Child Abuse and Neglect (NIS–4): Report to Congress. Washington, National Incidence Study of Child Abuse and Neglect (NIS–4): Report to Congress. Washington, DC: U.S. Department of Health and Human Services, Administration for Children and Families.

Silverman, A., Reinherz, H. & Giaconia, R. (1996). The long-term sequelae of child and adolescent abuse: A longitudinal study. *Child abuse & neglect*, 20 (8), pp. 709-723.

Smith, M., & Segal, J. (2017). *Child abuse and neglect*. Retrieved from https://www.helpguide.org/articles/abuse/child-abuse-and-neglect.htm

Smith, M., Robinson, L., Segal, R., & Segal, J. (2018). *Post-traumatic stress disorder (ptsd)*. Retrieved from https://www.helpguide.org/articles/ptsd-trauma/ptsd-symptoms-self-help-treatment.htm#what

Summary: Foster care (n.d.). Retrieved from http://www.kidsdata.org/topic/4/foster-care/summary?gclid=Cj0KEQjw5ti3BRD89aDFnb3SxPcBEiQAssnp0vZ5CKfxDRyHh

10 Signs of Child Abuse (n.d.). Retrieved from http://www.safehorizon.org/page/10-signs-of-child-abuse-58.html

Tennyson Center for Children. (n.d.). *How to recognize child abuse*. Retrieved from https://www.tennysoncenter.org/about-child-abuse/

The Children's Assessment Center. (n.d.). *Child sexual abuse facts*. Retrieved from http://cahouston.org/child-sexual-abuse-facts/

The First Society for the Prevention of Cruelty to Animals (n.d.). Retrieved from http://www.spcai.org/about-spcai/our-history/

The NY Society for the Prevention of Cruelty to Children (n.d.). Retrieved from http://www.nyspcc.org/

Trauma-informed care for children exposed to violence: Tips for Teachers (n.d.). Office of Juvenile Justice and Delinquency Prevention. Retrieved from http://www.safestartcenter.org

U.S. Department of Health & Human Services, Administration for Children and Families, Administration on Children, Youth and Families, Children's Bureau. (2016). *Child Maltreatment 2014*. Retrieved from http://www.acf.hhs.gov/programs/cb/research-data-technology/statistics-research/child-maltreatment

US Department of Health and Human Services, Administration on Children, Youth and Families (2009). *Child Maltreatment 2007*. Washington, DC: US Government Printing Office.

What are traumatic stress symptoms in pediatric patients and families (n.d.). Retrieved from https://www.healthcaretoolbox.org/what-providers-need-to-know/sign-a-symptoms?

MORE RESOURCES:

Scenarios:
Virginia DSS:
http://www.dss.virginia.gov/family/cps/mandated_reporters/cwse5691/story_html5.htmlCobb
County, Georgia Schools:
http://www.cobbk12.org/childabusereport/How to talk to kids:
https://www.virtuallabschool.org/management/child-abuse-id-reporting/lesson-2

New York State Information:
https://cfn201.wikispaces.com/file/view/Mandated+Reporter+Training.pdf
http://nysmandatedreporter.org/

Excellent Websites for Information:
www.childabuse.org
www.preventchldabuseny.org
www.nyspcc.org
www.cdc.gov
www.ChildTrauma.org
http://americanspcc.org
www.childhelp.org
https://www/joyfulheartfoundation.org
www.nationalchildrensalliance.org
www.helpguide.org
https://rainn.org
Child Welfare Information Gateway: https://www.childwelfare.gov

Printed in the USA
CPSIA information can be obtained
at www.ICGtesting.com
LVHW080810270824
789339LV00005B/47